**This book is to be returned on or before
the last date stamped below.**

13. NOV. 1984		
-3. FEB. 1986		
-4. JUN. 1986		
-6. JAN. 1987		
11. APR. 1994		
-9. MAY 1994		
31. OCT. 1994		
28. NOV. 1994		
22. OCT. 2003		
10.		
23. 2010		
23. 2		

LOFTS

Anne Boleyn

ENDPAPERS A cushion cover from the
sixteenth century embroidered in wool
and silk

FRONTISPIECE Anne Boleyn. The
'Devil's Pawmark' can be seen below her
right ear

Anne Boleyn

Defiled is my name, full sore
Through cruel spite and false report
That I may say for evermore,
Farewell to joy, adieu comfort.

Norah Lofts

Orbis Publishing, London

This book was designed and produced by
George Rainbird Limited,
36 Park Street, London W1Y 4DE

ISBN: 0 85613 242 X

House Editor: Elizabeth Blair
Designer: Gail Engert
Picture Researcher: Alison Catling
Indexer: Irene Clephane

The text was set and printed and the book bound
by Jarrold & Sons Ltd, Norwich, Norfolk
The colour plates and jacket were originated by
Gilchrist Bros. Ltd, Leeds, West Yorkshire

Printed in Great Britain

Contents

Colour Plates

The page numbers given are those opposite
the colour plates, or, in the case of a
double-page spread, those either side
of the plate.

Anna Bollein Queen.

I

Hever and France

In ancient shadows and twilights
Where childhood has strayed,
The world's great sorrows were born
And its hero's made.
In the lost boyhood of Judas
Christ was betrayed.

A.E. (George Russell)

When Anne Boleyn was born she was of so little importance that nobody bothered to record the date or the place of her birth. When she died everyone knew the place, the date, the very hour. In the not-quite-certain space of time between the two events she had been Queen of England for three years bar a few days; she had been the centre of one of the most famous love-stories and the subject of the most outrageous scandal. She had been the direct cause of the severance of the Church of England from the Church of Rome, 'the cause and the principal wet-nurse of heresy'. Many men, some accused of being her lovers and others against whom such a charge could not possibly be brought, had died because of her. She had ruined a Queen's life and a King's disposition; and she had given birth to Queen Elizabeth, the most remarkable woman ever to wear a crown.

All this in how many years? Nobody is quite certain..

The *Encyclopaedia Britannica* dates her birth at about 1507; the *Dictionary of National Biography* says, firmly, 1504; Agnes Strickland – an authority on the Queens of England – arguing from internal evidence, suggests 1500 or even 1499; Friedmann who devoted two massive volumes to her biography, says 1502 or 1503. Other writers vary just as widely: she is said to have been fourteen when Henry was first attracted to her in 1523; or that she was a slip of a girl of sixteen at that same date.

OPPOSITE Anne Boleyn sketched by Holbein

Blickling Hall, Norfolk, the probable birthplace of Anne Boleyn

Ordinarily a few years this way or that would matter little, but one must bear in mind that Henry VIII, infatuated by her in 1523, was determined to marry her in 1527, and no matter how deep his infatuation, the begetting of an heir was always his first concern. He knew that even if the business of getting a divorce from Katharine of Aragon went as smoothly as he hoped, it would take some time. The difference in child-bearing potential between a girl of sixteen and a mature woman of twenty-three was considerable in an age when a woman was rather old at thirty, a man old at fifty.

Nothing in Anne's behaviour in and after that crucial year 1523 hints at the callowness of extreme youth, so let us take the middle of the road – usually regarded as the safest place – and suggest that she was eighteen when Henry first saw her as desirable and give her birthdate, tentatively, as 1505.

Where she was born matters far less. Two places claim her; Blickling Hall in Norfolk and Hever Castle in Kent. Both properties belonged to her father, Sir Thomas Boleyn, and though Hever Castle sounds grander, much of the castle had gone and both places were Tudor mansions of the kind acquired, not inherited, by up-and-coming people like the Boleyns.

As regards Anne's birthplace, the balance tips very slightly in favour of Blickling. The Boleyns were Norfolk-orientated and her grandparents were buried in the church at near-by Salle.

The Boleyns were not quite the upstarts that their enemies said them to be. They were not members of the old aristocracy, so diminished by the Yorkist-Lancastrian Wars which had only ended in 1485 when Henry VIII's father, Henry VII, had taken the throne of England and rather discouraged the great lords – potential trouble-makers, and encouraged the middle men – potential money-earners. Anne's great-grandfather was so successful in trade as a mercer, dealing in cloth, that he became master of his guild and eventually Lord Mayor of London. When he died he was able to leave £1,000, then a colossal sum, to the poor, and he had married a lady of noble birth. Anne's father did even better, in a worldly sense; owning Blickling and Hever and some minor properties, he could afford to become a courtier, and he made a very grand marriage, having as his wife Elizabeth Howard, daughter of the man who was to become the Duke of Norfolk. Of this marriage there were three children, Mary, Anne and George. There was some slight scandal about the Lady Elizabeth Boleyn and her extra-marital activities, and naturally this was revived and made much of when Anne's own behaviour was being maligned.

Of Anne's early life so little is known that there is argument even about whether her mother died when she was a child, or whether she outlived her by two years. What evidence there is – a sentence in a letter and a few words on a tombstone, suggest that Elizabeth Howard lived on until 1538, and that the stepmother of humble origin is part of the myth. Not that mother or stepmother would have made much difference to the little girl's upbringing; in Tudor times, though the child mortality rate made children precious, people who could afford hirelings, entrusted even the doubly precious boys to the care of wet-nurses, ordinary nurses, governors or governesses, and tutors. Sir Thomas Boleyn was exceptional in that he gave his second daughter a good education. She had a French governess, known as Simonette, so she grew up bilingual and could read and write at what seems to us an astonishingly early age. (But we must consider the whole background; Anne's daughter, Elizabeth, made her half-brother Edward a finely stitched shirt for his birthday when she was six. With life expectancy so short, there was no time to waste.)

Anne Boleyn was first publicly mentioned as being one of the attendant ladies who accompanied the King's sister, Mary Tudor, when she went to France in 1514, part of a package peace deal, to marry Louis XII of France.

Henry VIII attends the lists in state. He had an impressive reputation for his skill at jousting and other sports

Mary, very young and pretty, had agreed to marry Louis, an old man of fifty-two with bad health and bad teeth, with the utmost reluctance; but the marriage was of diplomatic importance, and she gave in, only stipulating that when Louis died she should be free to marry the man of her choice.

The mention of bad teeth is revealing. It is a seemingly little thing, but before the time when a bad tooth could be removed other than brutally by a blacksmith, there were bad teeth, even in the mouths of Kings; the resultant halitosis was a thing to be reckoned with. In fact Kings, negotiating for marriage with Princesses they had never seen, gave their envoys instructions to make certain of sweet breath. Princesses, naturally, could not afford such precautions.

Mary sailed in October and Henry and Katharine with a great number of courtiers went to Dover to see her off in style, for this was a grand match, one which old Henry VII had hoped for. As usual in October the weather was very windy and the sailing was delayed for several days, the Royal family lodging in Dover Castle. Then the wind abated slightly and embarkation could begin. So there on Dover beach, on a still-blustery

Sweet breath was an important attribute for a prospective marriage partner and tooth extraction was extremely painful in the sixteenth century

morning, four people whose destinies were interlocked came together.

There was Henry, twenty-three years old, very handsome, very regal. Even when he was a child, and merely a second son, there had been something about his demeanour and bearing which impressed people. He was over six feet tall in a time when the average height was less than it is today, and hard exercise kept him slim and taut. He had curling auburn hair, very blue eyes and a fresh complexion. He had inherited the looks, as well as many of the characteristics, of his Plantagenet grandfather, Edward IV. We are so accustomed to seeing him portrayed as a gross, guzzling, lecherous old man that it is necessary to remind ourselves that he was acknowledged to be the best-looking Royal person in Christendom — as well as the most learned and the most liberal-minded.

Beside him stood Katharine the Queen, almost six years his senior. She had come from Spain when she was fifteen to marry Arthur, Prince of Wales, who had died four months after the wedding. Pope Julius II had granted a dispensation for Henry to marry his brother's widow, and Henry had been romantically in love with her. It had been, on the whole, a happy marriage except that it had, so far, produced only one living child, a baby Prince who had died while the celebrations for his christening were still going on. It may be worth mentioning here that Katharine was exceedingly pious, and in the time between her betrothal to Henry and her marriage – a time when she was extremely unhappy and insecure because she knew that if a better match was offered Henry VII would have taken it, disregarding his son's feelings – she had practised such religious austerities that the Pope himself had feared for her health, and was concerned lest she should undermine her child-bearing ability. Regarding Henry as her husband – which shows how seriously the business of betrothal was sometimes taken, the Pope suggested he should forbid Katharine to fast so often, to spend such long hours on her knees in cold chapels. It is just possible that in this respect the Pope may have been right.

However in 1514 there was still hope of a living child for Henry and Katharine; and also for Mary Tudor and Louis XII.

As it happened Mary Tudor's marriage to Louis XII lasted as short a time as she had wished it to. Then she married, without bothering to ask her brother's consent, the man of her choice, Charles Brandon. And her children by that unauthorized marriage were to produce children who, through her, had a claim to the throne and gave trouble to Henry and Katharine's daughter, not yet born.

And there, on the windswept beach was Anne Boleyn, inconspicuous and unnoticed except that her name was jotted down, and in good company. Of the other three lady attendants named, two were bloodkin to the new Queen of France and one was a nobleman's daughter. Anne Boleyn was much honoured and she was grateful to her father for securing her the appointment, and she wrote to thank him. Sir Thomas Boleyn was very skilful in the art of infiltration; he had found a place for Mary in Brussels, with Margaret of Austria who was ruling the Netherlands, part of the unwieldy Habsburg Empire. Presently he would find a place at Court for George, and here was Anne, off to France where, if she acquired nothing else, she would gain polish, sophistication, style.

Much of the argument about her age centres on this date, 1514; there is the contention that no girl not yet in her teens could possibly have been considered as a lady-in-waiting of whom some purely symbolic duties and certain dignified behaviour would be expected. It is a valid argument, and the one upon which Miss Strickland bases her premise that Anne must have been at least in her early teens in 1514. However, in Tudor times,

OPPOSITE *Louis XII* by Jean Perréal, the portrait sent to Henry VIII in 1514 when Louis was seeking the hand of Mary Tudor in marriage

children-of-honour had their place in many courts, and even today many brides choose to be attended by very young bridesmaids. If Anne Boleyn was in fact only nine years old on that windy day on Dover beach, she had every qualification to be, if not a maid-of-honour, a child-of-honour. She was probably tall for her age – her height is frequently mentioned later; she was, by modern standards, precocious, and her French was better than average, thanks to Simonette. In the sphere of duty nothing very onerous would be expected of her since Mary, once she was Queen of France, would be surrounded by Frenchwomen.

Anyone bothering to look at this young maid-of-honour would have been struck by two things; her grace and her colouring. She had the slight build that makes for elegance, and an exceptionally long, slender neck. She is said to have had an extra cervical vertebra. (But how can anyone know that?) She had magnificent dark eyes – even her enemies admitted that – and a great wealth of black silky hair. She lacked that thing so closely associated with beauty that the word "fair" in itself implies beauty; she was not fair. Those who wished to decry her called her complexion sallow, a word with an unpleasant sound; it was probably of an unvarying creaminess, the kind of skin least affected by wind or weather – or emotion. At a great crisis in her life it was observed that her colour did not change.

She had two flaws; on that long slender neck a mole, said to be the size of a strawberry, and described by one of her detractors as 'a great wen', and on her right hand a rudimentary sixth finger of which, again, much is made by those who disliked her. The grandson of a man who knew her very well wrote that it was only 'some little show of a nail'. It was something which she could keep concealed by the tip of the next finger. (Her daughter, Queen Elizabeth, was justly proud of her hands which were of an elegance hardly ever seen; and it is more than likely that she inherited these from her mother whose name she would never speak.)

Young Mary Tudor's wish was granted. The distasteful marriage lasted only a very short time and early in 1515 she was a widow. Henry sent one of his best friends, Charles Brandon, to escort her home; with indecent haste and in great secrecy, they were married. Henry was furious. A Dowager Queen of France, a Princess of England, very pretty and not yet eighteen, could have been used to advantage in the political marriage

OPPOSITE Anne Boleyn became Henry VIII's second wife in 1533 and three years later met her death on the executioner's block

ANNA BOLINA VXOR ⋅ HENRI ⋅ OCTA

market; yet he soon forgave Mary and her husband, and created Brandon
Duke of Suffolk, an act of magnanimity which shows what kind of man he
was before his nature was warped. For Mary it was not a happy choice:
Brandon was notorious for his infidelities.

Anne did not return to England; she became one of the household of
Queen Claude, wife of Francis I. Claude's character much resembled that
of Katharine of Aragon; she was intensely pious and ruled, somebody
said, over a nunnery rather than a Court. Anne had again been very
privileged, for every great family in France was eager to send its daughters
to be trained by the good Queen. How long Anne remained in that sedate

ABOVE Mary Tudor married Charles Brandon in secret after the death of her first
husband, Louis XII
OPPOSITE Henry VIII, after Holbein

atmosphere is uncertain; we hear of her next in a more lively place, the household of the Duchess of Alençon, the King's sister, Marguerite, where the emphasis was less upon piety than accomplishment, not only in music and dancing but in that indefinable thing called style, in dress, in speech, in wit. To the end of her life those who disliked Anne complained that she was Frenchified.

In 1520 came that great summit meeting between Henry of England and Francis of France, known as 'the Field of the Cloth of Gold'. The two young men – born to be rivals – were very curious about each other. They had much in common; both were young, ambitious, energetic, both of superb physique, Francis a shade taller, Henry decidedly better-looking. Their meeting was arranged and organized by Wolsey, the great Minister whom Henry had inherited from his father. Wolsey and Henry fitted perfectly. Henry had had a dull youth, endless lessons on every subject under the sun, and supervision so strict that from the age of thirteen until he came to the throne just as he was eighteen, he had occupied rooms which could only be reached through his father's and needed permission to leave the premises of whatever palace was being occupied at the moment. At the same time he had been kept in absolute ignorance of anything to do with government. When he became King, he wanted to have fun and enjoy his freedom, his marriage to the Princess of his adolescent dreams, and there was Wolsey, thirty-nine years old, infinitely experienced, with an insatiable appetite for work, a positive hunger for responsibility and power, only too ready to tell Henry to leave everything to him and go away and enjoy himself.

Wolsey was a Francophile; he liked all things French, even the cooking, and he felt that it was time that the Francophobia of most Englishmen – a hangover of the Hundred Years War – should be ended by an understanding between near neighbours and an alliance against any enemy. As a statesman, Wolsey was worried about the balance of power in Europe, about the size, the vast territories and wealth of what was called 'the Empire'. The territory, some gained by war, more by careful marriages, belonged to the Habsburg family, but the title of Emperor went by election. There was a time when Henry VIII aspired to it, just as Wolsey hoped to be elected Pope. In theory both things were possible; in practice the title of Pope tended to gravitate to Italian candidates – in all

OPPOSITE *Francis I* by Jean Clouet. Henry met Francis in 1520 at the Field of the Cloth of Gold, a meeting arranged and organized by Wolsey

history only one Englishman had attained it – and the title of Emperor was practically the prerogative of the Habsburg family.

The Emperor, when Henry and Francis were young, was young, too, but not young as they were young. Because his mother had been Katharine of Aragon's sister, Queen of Castile in her own right, and his grandfather, Ferdinand of Aragon, had died heirless, Charles V had added the whole of Spain, and through Spain, all the New World to his already vast Empire. Charles's mother had been demonstrably mad; he was not, but he had inherited a deep streak of melancholy which was eventually to engulf him and make him renounce the world which had given him so much. His great Empire most nearly affected England because it included the Netherlands, and trade between England where sheep flourished and the lower, damper Netherlands where they did not, had always been brisk and two-sided. England sent wool to the Netherlands, where it was made into cloth, and England imported the cloth. The two communities lived, so to speak, by taking in each other's washing. But Wolsey, in some ways farsighted, could see that if at any time the French and Charles V cared to combine against England in one of those silly differences which could lead to war, England's position would be hopeless. He wanted a firm alliance with the French.

But even while the Field of the Cloth of Gold was being planned, Henry and Katharine were entertaining Charles in a quiet, unostentatious fashion. Charles was Katharine's nephew, and everything was done to make his visit seem to be simply a family affair of no political significance; in fact it concerned the betrothal of Charles to Katharine's one living child, a daughter, Mary, born in 1516. The idea of a marriage between a young man aged twenty-one and a child of four was absurd, but it was an idea very dear to Katharine's heart and Charles pretended to consider the matter seriously because he wanted England as an ally against France. Not surprisingly, he later backed out of this betrothal and married one of his Portuguese cousins, of child-bearing age and the owner of a dowry worth £1,000,000. (This abortive attempt to marry Mary to the Emperor only touches Anne Boleyn in that at the time some of the Emperor's lawyers did raise the question of whether Mary, child of a possibly incestuous marriage, could be regarded as strictly legitimate and, therefore, heiress to England. Henry knew that the question had been raised, and although he did nothing about it at the time, it would be wrong to say that the validity

OPPOSITE *Charles V* by Titian. Charles was the nephew of Katharine of Aragon and a staunch supporter of her claim to be the rightful Queen of Henry VIII

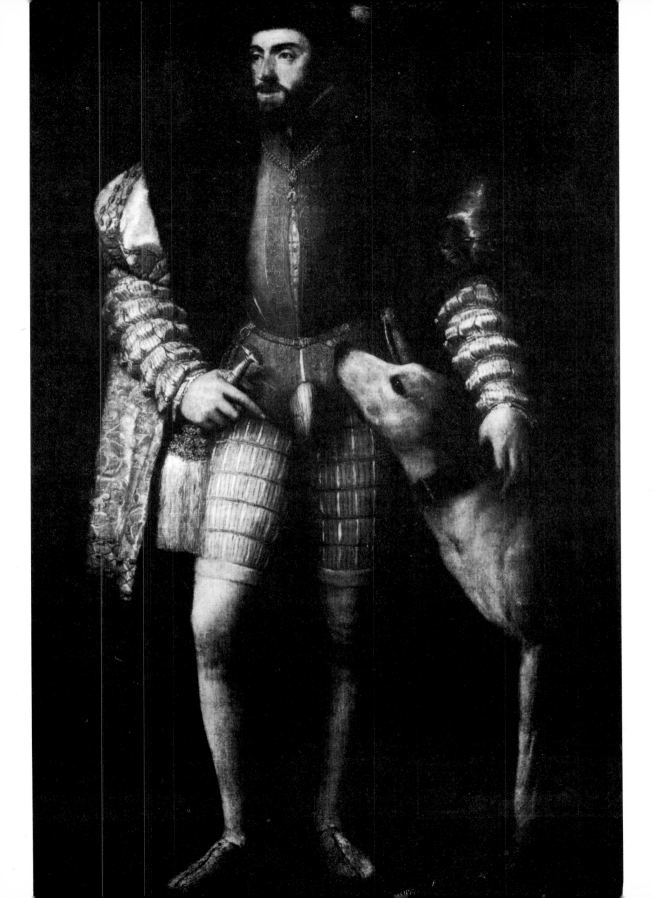

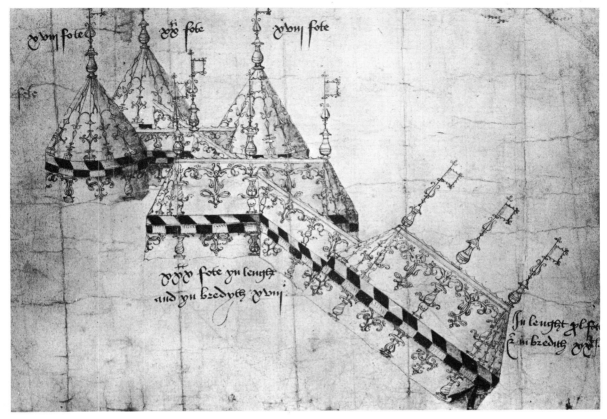

ABOVE Design by Richard Gibson for the tents that were erected at the Field of the Cloth of Gold
OPPOSITE Shearing the woollen cloth that formed such an important trade link with the Netherlands in the sixteenth century

of his marriage had never been questioned until he became enchanted by Anne. And it is almost certain that had Katharine produced a son, Henry would never have tried to rid himself of Katharine, however deep his infatuation for another woman. He had taken the sex of his first healthy child well, saying she would have brothers. Although often pregnant, Katharine had as often miscarried, and in the year of the Field of the Cloth of Gold, she was thirty-six. Her child-bearing time was running out.)

By entertaining Charles immediately before meeting Francis, and by going on to see him again immediately afterwards, Henry was almost ensuring that the Field of the Cloth of Gold would result in nothing sincere or permanent. It became a wonderful spectacle, an exercise in competitiveness. To do Francis justice he suggested that too much show and grandeur should be avoided, but both Henry and Wolsey liked show and grandeur; so in a valley not far from Calais there sprang up vast faked palaces made of board painted to look like brickwork, lined throughout

From a stone relief in the Hotel Bourgtheroulde at Rouen showing the meeting of Francis I and Henry VIII at the Field of the Cloth of Gold on 7 June 1520

with the costliest of hangings, splendidly furnished, 'the last great canvas of the Middle Ages'. Thousands of workmen were employed to build and gild and fix real glass windows in the makeshift walls. There were fountains offering red wine, white wine and fresh water in silver cups for all comers. And because Wolsey was a churchman, there was a particularly splendid chapel with an organ of silver, and solid gold statues of the Twelve Apostles, each the size of a twelve-year-old child. Wolsey's own special singing boys provided the choir, and with his care for detail, he took reserves, in case some boy's voice should break or he should erupt with the pimples of puberty. It was in this chapel that Queen Katharine and Queen Claude were so anxious each to give precedence to the other that a whole ceremony was delayed.

Sir Thomas Boleyn was certainly among the 4,544 persons who made up the King of England's retinue. Was Anne there with the Duchess of Alençon's ladies? If so, she attracted no notice.

At the end of sixteen days, with exchanges of ostentatious hospitality and extravagant entertainments, the summit meeting ended, with one English lord speaking for others when he said that he hoped that if he ever had to meet a Frenchman again, it would be at a sword's point. And although it was high summer, a great storm sprang up and wrecked the fake palaces and the silk pavilions before they could be dismantled. It was symbolic: for within two years, England and France were at war again. And Anne Boleyn came home.

2

The Spell is Cast

As the holly groweth green with ivy all alone
When flowers cannot be seen; and greenwood leaves be gone,
So unto my lady promise to her I make
From all other only to her I me take.

Henry VIII to Anne Boleyn

Anne came home partly because of the war and partly because her father
had plans for her. Through his mother, Margaret Butler, Sir Thomas had
some claim to the Butler titles, one English, one Irish, which, like so many
others, were the subject of dispute because of the Civil War between York
and Lancaster. Margaret Butler has been a co-heiress and another branch
of the family, with male heirs, had contested Sir Thomas's claim. Henry
VIII had prudently put off any decision because the Butlers were in
Ireland, where England needed friends, not enemies. So there was a
compromise; Sir Thomas might not be given the titles he so much
coveted, but Anne could marry the young Butler heir.

   This scheme may have been brewing in Sir Thomas's mind for some
time and would account for the fact that in an age of early betrothals, no
plans had been made for a girl, neither deformed nor demented, and on
one side of her family at least, well connected. That in itself is
extraordinary; and even more remarkable is the fact that talented, lively,
and if not beautiful in the accepted sense, definitely attractive, she had
attracted no offer of marriage – or least none that we hear of – while she
was in France. Until the war broke out in 1523, Sir Thomas was often in
France, on this errand and that, and it is possible that he had told Anne and
others that he had plans for her. This is pure conjecture, but it might
explain why she came back to England completely unattached, a free
subject for a bargain – which fell through. Sir Piers Butler, suspecting,
probably correctly, that this marriage of Anne Boleyn to his son was

OPPOSITE Henry VIII

King Henry the eyght.

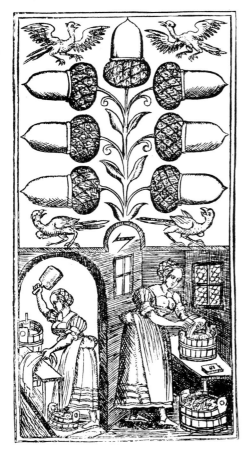 

ABOVE Playing cards. Although Katharine of Aragon was pious, her Court was not dull and she herself was fond of card games

OPPOSITE The parliament of Henry VIII. As the break with the Church of Rome came nearer, Henry grew more dependent on the opinion of his parliament

merely an excuse for keeping his son in England, more or less as a hostage for his own good behaviour in Ireland, promptly ordered his son home. Sir Thomas was disappointed, but, using his influence, managed to get Anne a place at Court as one of the Queen's waiting ladies.

Katharine was pious, but her Court was far from dull. She herself was fond of rich clothing and jewels; she enjoyed playing cards, gambling for modest stakes; she liked gay, well-dressed, accomplished young women about her, and suitable young men such as were found in the King's household, and in Wolsey's, were always welcome to come and join in the music, the dancing and the masques.

As the daughter of a mere knight, Anne's status was low in a place where rank was of paramount importance, deciding as it did the quality of the apartments a lady was allotted, how many personal servants she was allowed, whether she might have her own horse or not, and, of course, who preceded whom through any doorway. Later people were to complain of Anne's arrogance, and this may have stemmed, in part, from past humiliations. She may even have been comparatively poor; nothing much in her father's record suggests that he was a generous man. However, she had not been at Court long before her prospects became very bright indeed; she attracted the attention of a most eligible young man, Lord Henry Algernon Percy, heir to the Earl of Northumberland. He had been sent, as was the custom of the day, to be educated and trained in Wolsey's household, and whenever the Cardinal went to Court, young Percy 'would resort for his pastime unto the Queen's chamber and there fall into dalliance with the Queen's maidens'. It was soon noticeable that of them all, he favoured Anne Boleyn the most. She favoured him, too, and was later heard to say that she would sooner have been Harry's Countess than Henry's Queen.

But another eye had seen and approved of her. Why else should the King fly into a temper when he heard of this growing attachment and order Wolsey to put a stop to it at once? Admittedly there was a difference in rank, but Henry had condoned his sister's marriage to a commoner, and he had it in his power to make, with a flick of the finger, Sir Thomas Boleyn an Earl too – he actually did so a few years later.

Wolsey, of course, acted at once. He believed that a scolding from him would be enough; after all, though he was Henry's faithful servant, internationally he was regarded as the real ruler of England; and all he had to deal with here was a young man suffering an attack of calf-love.

Wolsey did not even bother to be tactful; he administered his rebuke in the presence of others, saying that he marvelled greatly that Harry Percy should be such a fool as to contemplate marriage with Anne Boleyn, a mere knight's daughter, when his own prospects were so high: 'After thy father's death thou art likely to inherit and enjoy one of the noblest Earldoms in this kingdom.'

Did ever a young lover heed such an argument? Harry Percy did not. He answered back; he mentioned Anne's mother and grandmother, both so well-born. That he should have bothered with her lineage was a sign that he was serious in his intentions. He was so stubborn – Wolsey used the word 'wilful' – that in the end all the great Cardinal could do was to send for the wilful boy's father.

The Earl of Northumberland came roaring down from the North, travelling more lightly than he had done when, going to a now-forgotten war, he took with him a feather bed, cushions of silk, twelve silver dishes, twelve silver spoons, six saucers. Such display was suitable for a great lord

Letter from Henry VIII to Cardinal Wolsey thanking him for his
devotion to the King's business. It ends with the words 'Wryttyn with
the hand of your lovyng master HENRY R.'

going to war, less suitable for a man coming to rebuke a wilful son, and in
rather a shaky personal position. The Earl of Northumberland had
offended Henry VII and had been fined £10,000, a stupendous sum; he
had paid about a tenth of the amount, the rest had been suspended, but
could be called in at any moment by Henry VIII who had inherited
everything that his father had owned. The Earl of Northumberland knew
that whatever was asked of him he must do or be virtually ruined.

He had a brief, private talk with Wolsey and emerged with an
irrefutable argument; Harry could not possibly marry Anne Boleyn
because he was already betrothed to Lady Mary Talbot, a daughter of the

Earl of Shrewsbury. In the face of such argument, and under the threat that he would be disinherited unless he gave in, Harry Percy succumbed. He is said to have wept, which may sound unmanly, but the Tudors were uninhibited; we read of many men in tears over a far less serious business. Separation from Anne undoubtedly ruined Harry Percy's life. He honoured the betrothal contract – about which he knew nothing until his father hurled the information at him – and he and his wife lived most unhappily. Possibly the marriage was not even consummated. On one occasion Mary Talbot complained that he did not behave as a husband to her, and he retorted that he was not her husband because he had been pre-contracted to Anne Boleyn. Finally his wife went home to her father, and Harry, by this time sixth Earl of Northumberland, died young. *Burke's Peerage*, that meticulous handbook, does not give the date of his birth, only of his death, January 1537. He survived his lost love by seven months. The way in which he was treated in 1523 suggests that he was not more than twenty at the time.

Charged with no specific offence, Anne was ordered to leave Court and return home to Hever. She blamed Wolsey for everything and swore that if ever it lay in her power she would work the Cardinal as much displeasure as he had done her. At the time it sounded the idlest of idle threats.

Recorded history is so full of gaps. We know that Anne went back to Hever broken-hearted and in a flaming bad temper. We can only guess at how she was received there. Everything we know about Thomas Boleyn leads us to suspect that he was sadly disappointed in Anne, as he had been in his other daughter, Mary. He had done his best for them both. Mary, too, had been schooled on the Continent and gained herself a bad reputation – afterwards to be used in the slanderous campaign against Anne. Mary may have been the mistress of Francis I for a short time; she had certainly been Henry VIII's mistress, but from that advantageous position she had gained nothing, either for herself or her family. She had not persuaded her Royal lover to grant Sir Thomas one of the titles he coveted; she had asked no favours for herself; she was still nothing but the wife of William Carey, a man of moderate means and a fairly undistinguished member of the King's household.

Anne had done no better; she had simply indulged in a flirtation with a young man not free to marry her and lost her place at Court. One must

OPPOSITE Hever Castle, Kent, the home of Anne Boleyn. It was here that Henry first saw Anne and fell in love with her

Mary Boleyn by Holbein. Henry had taken Mary briefly as his mistress before she married Sir William Carey

imagine Hever Castle in the early autumn of 1523 as a dismal centre of frustration with Anne taking refuge in the ailments now recognized as psychosomatic.

Then, in late October, the King came to Hever, making a sudden, unannounced, informal visit. And all was changed.

Such a visit was uncharacteristic of Henry. When he visited one of his subjects he went royally, expecting a Royal reception. And if he wanted to confer with Sir Thomas on any matter, the briefest word would have brought the courtier to London. Sir Thomas used Hever more than he did Blickling because it was within easier reach of the city.

OPPOSITE Thomas Boleyn, Earl of Wiltshire and Ormonde, by Holbein

Sir Thomas Boleyn welcomes Henry VIII to Hever Castle while Anne watches from an upstairs window

So, what was afoot? Sir Thomas, not unskilled in putting two and two together, made a hit-or-miss guess at the truth and ordered Anne to go to bed and stay there until the King had gone.

Henry was then thirty-two years old and since he became King, had always had his own way except in the matter of children. Wolsey and every other official had seen that his wishes were carried out, even forestalled if possible. Katharine prided herself on being the most obedient wife in the world. He had become like a spoiled child, and like a spoiled child found anything just out of reach irresistible, the one thing desirable. It is more than likely that had Anne been as available as Mary had been, had Sir Thomas been as conniving as he had been in Mary's case, the vagrant fancy, soon satisfied, would have burned itself out. As it was, it became a

Henry and Anne walk in the Long Gallery at Hever. Henry's visits to Anne became increasingly frequent as he fell more deeply under her spell

consuming passion, ready to sacrifice anything, everything, in order to attain its end.

The King came again to Hever, little thinking how often he would make that journey, how often he would go away baffled, or angry, but always more infatuated than ever.

He was himself to say later that he had been bewitched. Other people were to call Anne a witch, and indeed a faint, tantalizing whiff of magic does blow through the story now and again.

It was a credulous age. In Canterbury, in the Convent of St Sepulchre, there was at the time when Anne was moping at Hever, a nun, formerly a serving-girl who claimed to see visions, to foretell the future, to be in direct touch with God, through the mediumship of Mary Magdalene. She was a sixteenth-century Joan of Arc, though Joan communicated with St Catherine, the patron saint of virgins. Eventually Elizabeth Barton, the Holy Nun of Kent, was to suffer the same fate as Joan, but in the meantime she enjoyed great popularity, and not only with stupid, ignorant people. John Fisher, Bishop of Rochester, one of the bravest and most pious men of his generation visited her; so did Sir Thomas More, the most distinguished and honest lawyer in Christendom. It is true that More wrote her a sensible letter, telling her not to meddle in politics and that Fisher did not report – as Henry thought he should have done – all that she told him; but that two such men should go to see her and take notice of what she said, is a measure of the credulity of the age. And perhaps things have not changed much; we talk of telepathy, precognition, telekinesis, psychometry; and now and then we hear of a sheep's heart being nailed to a church door as a love-spell.

There are just a few things about Anne which merit a moment's wonder. She would be revenged upon Wolsey she said, if ever it lay in her power. How? He was one of the most powerful men in Europe, fabulously wealthy, infinitely cunning. She was a girl who had lost her suitor and been banished from Court, had no power of any kind and not a penny except what her miserly father chose to give her. Yet in the end she, and she alone, brought about the great Cardinal's fall.

Even in the Tower she made a typical witch's threat, saying that if she died there would be a seven-year drought in England. Witches claimed some control over the weather, and seven has always been regarded as a magic number.

She bore on her body two marks then commonly associated with witchcraft; the mole, sometimes called the 'Devil's Pawmark', and the slight deformity of the hand – these, of course, for the ignorant, were evidence enough, but cannot be seriously considered.

What remains is her behaviour. One is bound to ask oneself: *How did she dare?* She knew as well as anyone how urgent was Henry's need – England's need – for an heir; yet, told flatly that Henry's divorce would have gone through easily had he chosen some other woman to be his second wife, and there were plenty of candidates around, she held out. She would be Queen or nothing. She knew that he was fickle, headstrong, all-powerful, and at times not over-scrupulous, yet between that first visit of his to Hever in the autumn of 1523, and her admitting him to her bed in the autumn of 1532 she seemed never to doubt her power over him. Sometimes she did not even bother to be amiable. She nagged and scolded and gave free rein to her temper. For four years she resisted his appeals that she should return to Court where he could see her more easily and more often. To this kind of treatment he responded by being more devoted than ever, loading her with gifts, writing love-songs, and – always a most reluctant letter-writer – sending her some of the most ardent love-letters ever penned. He was a highly sexed man, in his prime, yet his behaviour never gave her cause for jealousy or alarm. He was, as he wrote, completely hers, a humble and obedient servant.

He must have soon realized that in order to possess her, he must

The accusation of witchcraft was often levelled at Anne to explain the strange hold she had over Henry. Witches claim to have some control over the weather and here witches conjure up rain with spells and magic potions

Fortune-telling by tarot cards

sacrifice much that he valued highly – including his dignity, yet he never wavered. He acted throughout like a man under a spell, and Anne behaved with what appeared to be superhuman assurance. It is significant, too, that once the spell was broken, having lasted for ten years, he reacted violently, passing from adoration to hatred with no intermittent stages, as though the spell had been suddenly lifted.

Those who like to think of Anne as a witch point out that she possessed an extraordinarily devoted wolfhound to whom she gave the name Urian – one of Satan's many names and virtually unknown to the uninitiated. Those who criticize everything she did say that Urian's docility was the result of being whipped. But the Tudors were not sentimental about animals and physical chastisement was used not only on four-legged animals but on children and servants. Anne had another dog, a small one, briefly mentioned. It met with an accident and died an untimely death: nobody dared to tell her for fear of the emotional scene which would result. It was left for Henry to break the news.

If she did indeed dabble in witchcraft, Anne Boleyn's end came in traditional pattern – let down and deserted by Satan, the Father of Lies. Also perhaps worth mentioning is the belief that the practice of sorcery was regarded as passing from mother to daughter; and there is that same slight yet better documented whiff of it in Elizabeth's reign. Elizabeth frequently resorted to Doctor Dee, a magician; she even allowed him to dictate, in consultation with the stars, her Coronation day, the one day which would ensure her a long and successful reign. She had a long and successful reign, against all odds – but she had a bad end too.

About such things nobody can be certain. We can only know that Anne refused to become Henry's mistress and eventually became his Queen.

3

Queen or Nothing

I have been waiting long, and might in the meantime have
contracted some advantageous marriage, out of which I might
have had issue, which is the greatest consolation in this world;
but alas! farewell to my time and youth bent to no purpose at all.

Anne Boleyn to Henry VIII

For an example of what a determined woman could achieve, Anne did not
have to look far; no further back in history than Henry's own
grandmother, the first commoner to become Queen of England. Her
name was Elizabeth Woodville and Edward IV had wished to make her
his mistress. She had made her famous and effective retort, 'My liege, I
know I am not good enough to be your Queen, but I am far too good to be
your mistress.' When Anne was saying much the same thing to Henry,
Elizabeth Woodville, who had become Queen, had been dead only just
over thirty years. (And curiously, there had been that same whiff of magic
there, Elizabeth Woodville's mother being commonly regarded as a
witch.)

There were similarities between Elizabeth Woodville and Anne
Boleyn, both ambitious, both resolute in virtue until the moment to yield
came; but there was one enormous, crucial difference. Edward IV had
been a bachelor; Henry VIII was married to Katharine whom he had once
loved and still respected, the woman with whom he had sorrowed over
the death of their one live-born son, rejoiced over the birth of a living
daughter, grieved over the subsequent miscarriages.

Katharine had been, in all but one respect, the ideal wife, tolerant even
of his occasional infidelities. She understood the temptations to which

OPPOSITE Katharine of Aragon, 1485–1536
OVERLEAF Field of the Cloth of Gold, 1520. Henry VIII can be seen in the bottom
left-hand corner accompanied by Wolsey as they ride towards the temporary palaces
erected for the meeting between Henry VIII and Francis I

CARDINAL WOOLSE

Kings were subjected and how easily women were seduced. Her father, Ferdinand of Aragon, had been married to a woman whom everybody admitted was the most wonderful woman in the world, yet he had been a womanizer of no mean order. Isabella had made no fuss, and her daughter, Katharine, had made no fuss over Henry's two recorded infidelities. Henry had been, in fact, for a King in his time, surprisingly moderate, and very discreet in his womanizing. He had had a mistress called Bessie Blount, one of Katharine's waiting women, but he had not flaunted her in front of his wife and his visits to her had been decently disguised. In 1519 Bessie Blount had borne a son, proving that, bedded with another woman, Henry could beget a boy, a thing which must have cut Katharine to the heart. Then, but briefly, Henry had taken Mary Boleyn as his mistress. He may have had a few other very casual affairs about which nothing was said; all his servants and close attendants had been warned not to gossip about him. His wooing of Anne Boleyn could, however, not remain a secret for long. Henry, in the effort to please her, showered favours upon her father, making him a Knight of the Garter, giving him one of the titles he longed for – Viscount Rochford, sending him as Ambassador to the Emperor and appointing him to a number of posts which carried financial rewards. Even George Boleyn was not overlooked, and he was given a Norfolk manor. And still, having taken her stand, Anne was not to be budged.

Henry wrote songs in her praise and sang them to her, accompanying himself on the lute. Nothing touched her. She had soon realized that he had been responsible for the breaking off of her affair with Harry Percy and in the early stages, at least, resentment would stiffen her resistance; and though later on, when her plan was made, she might pretend to love him it is doubtful whether she ever did so. She may have been one of those rare women who love once and never again; she may even have been undersexed as so many skilled flirts are.

We cannot know exactly when, or in what words, Anne informed him that she must be Queen or nothing; we do know that she was back in Court in May 1527 and that Henry was showing her marked attention even on such a formal occasion as a reception of French Ambassadors come to talk about Princess Mary's marriage to a French Prince and in the middle of that month Henry took his first secret steps towards getting rid of Katharine. This business is usually referred to as a divorce but that is a

OPPOSITE Cardinal Wolsey, 1475–1530

LEFT Prince Arthur, Henry's brother and first husband to Katharine of Aragon
RIGHT Elizabeth Woodville, the wife of Edward IV, and the first commoner to
become Queen of England
OPPOSITE Music for a song composed by Henry VIII as a young man. He wrote many
songs for Anne and sang them to her himself

misnomer; divorce postulates the existence of a marriage while what
Henry set out to prove and make everyone agree to was that he had, in
fact, never been married at all.

Katharine of Aragon had come from Spain to marry Henry's elder
brother Arthur, slightly younger than she and small for his age. She was
fair and pretty and the English had taken her to their hearts, not least
because the match was so flattering to the nation as a whole. England was
a small, poor country, slowly recovering from a devastating Civil War,
and Henry VII was the first of his dynasty. For England to be linked with
Spain, then great and powerful, was a marvellous thing. The marriage

lasted four months and Katharine always declared that it had not been consummated because of Arthur's youth and failing health. After a lot of sordid bargaining which, since it does not concern Anne need not detain us, it was agreed to betroth the young widow to the new Prince of Wales. But, because she had been his brother's wife, such a marriage would be consanguineous, and needed a Papal Dispensation to make it legal.

Such Dispensations were easily come by. Popes realized that royalty must marry royalty and that some interbreeding was inevitable. Two of Katharine's sisters had in turn married the King of Portugal. The Pope was God's representative on earth and could, if he wished, authorize marriages far more incestuous than one between a man and his brother's widow. Julius II gave the Dispensation. Now Henry was questioning the validity of his marriage, bearing hard upon a text in Leviticus which said that a man should not marry his deceased brother's wife, for if he did they would be childless, and ignoring a contrary text in Deuteronomy which said that a man should marry his dead brother's wife and rear children in his name. (One hesitates to point a moral, but it is fact that the Bible is a very controversial book indeed and until the art of printing was introduced to England by Caxton and the Bible translated by Tyndale, most people were spared the agonizing which close study of it brings about. 'The Devil can cite Scripture for his purpose', as Shakespeare, who knew everything, said.)

Henry cited Leviticus and his troubled conscience in a secret little court, called together, by his own request, to accuse him of making an incestuous marriage. Wolsey was there, anxious only to please his King and visualising another, more fruitful marriage for him with a young French Princess, Renée. And the Archbishop of Canterbury, William Warham, was there – he had long ago expressed doubts about the validity of the marriage. There were lawyers there, too, some to accuse, some to defend the King of this concocted charge, for after all if he had been living in sin with Katharine, he had done so openly for eighteen years. And although to a King a marriage without a son might be tantamount to being childless, Mary's existence, the short life of the little boy, dead before his navel healed, even the miscarriages, seemed to prove that the Levitical curse of childlessness did not apply here. All the same, this small, secret, entirely English court was prepared to say that there was some doubt about the marriage. That doubt they would convey to the Pope –

OPPOSITE William Warham, the Archbishop of Canterbury, who had serious doubts about the validity of Katharine's first marriage to Prince Arthur

amus Arch Bp Cant

'The stoning of the Pope by the four evangelists' by Girolamo de Treviso. Avarice and hypocrisy lie beside the Pope

Julius was dead and Clement reigned in his place, and Clement would undoubtedly be accommodating.

But in this round, Henry, Wolsey, Warham, but most of all Anne, were unlucky. Even as the little court's decision was to be passed on to the Pope, Clement was just managing to save his life by scurrying from the Vatican by underground tunnels to the strong old Castle of St Angelo while the German soldiers of the Emperor were rampaging through Rome, raping nuns and mutilating priests. It was ironic that Charles, the most pious Catholic, at war against the French, should have been obliged

Francis I (left) and Pope Clement VII (right). Francis advised the Pope to declare Henry's marriage null and void

to employ troops from the Lutheran North. The Emperor himself was not there and the soldiers who committed the atrocities and looted the Eternal City were actually mutinous, taking orders from no one. Still, they were the forces of the Emperor and Clement, though unharmed, was a prisoner. It was unlikely, in the circumstances, that he would risk offending the Emperor by giving Henry permission to put away Katharine, who was his aunt. It was, indeed, dubious whether any message from England could even reach Clement.

However, this was the kind of situation which found Wolsey at his best, shrewd, self-confident, resourceful. He saw a chance to turn the disaster into an asset; the Pope would need friends now and might turn to England and, wishing to please Henry, agree to cancel Julius's Dispensation. And there was an alternative; while Clement was a prisoner he might hand over his duties and his authority to a council of Cardinals, of which Wolsey would be one; and Wolsey did not doubt his own power to cajole and bully his fellows into his way of thinking.

Wolsey still deluded himself with the belief that once free, Henry would marry Princess Renée. He knew of Anne Boleyn's existence, of course, had seen her return to Court in beautiful, costly clothes and glittering jewels, but he thought that she was – or was about to be – Henry's *maîtresse en titre* in the French style.

The first thing to do was to make contact with the Pope. Wolsey chose three men, already in or near Rome, to bribe their way into St Angelo. The scheme could have worked had not Henry made a colossal blunder.

He chose Doctor Knight as his own messenger to Clement, an ageing, not very competent man who was to bribe his way in also, and present some very curious requests indeed. Henry asked for his present marriage to be declared null and void; he asked for a Dispensation to allow him to marry a woman related to him by some degree of consanguinity – this related to his liaison with Mary Boleyn which in clerical eyes made Anne a relative; he asked for permission to marry a woman who had been contracted to another man but never slept with him – this related to Harry Percy; and he asked permission to commit bigamy. Added to these requests Henry, very hopeful now that he had persuaded Anne back to Court, asked permission to marry a woman with whom he had already had sexual intercourse. To add to Clement's confusion, came a letter from Katharine, begging that her case should be heard in Rome, and saying – as she was to say so often – that she had never been Arthur's wife in anything but name, so that there was no ground for an annulment.

Henry had taken upon himself the distasteful task of breaking to Katharine the news that the little private court presided over by Wolsey and Warham had found their marriage in doubt, and that his own conscience was much troubled and he was taking steps to put matters right. Katharine wept and her tears upset Henry who knew her to be a woman of great fortitude. So far as the shock of being asked to consider that one has lived in sin for eighteen years, and that one's child is a bastard could be eased, he tried to ease it, assuring her that she should always be well provided for and treated with honour as the Dowager Princess of Wales. But Katharine could see that no amount of kind treatment could

A walnut writing desk decorated with the heads of Henry VIII and Katharine of Aragon on the front

make Mary legitimate if both her parents regarded their marriage as illegal. It was essential that she should oppose the annulment; and to this, behind the tears, she was setting her mind like rock.

She had many arguments in her favour. She believed that Julius's Dispensation was sound; she was sure that her father and Henry's father, both very shrewd men, would not have agreed to a marriage about which there was the slightest doubt. And although she had prayed for and hoped for a son she could not agree that to have only a daughter was to be childless. She saw no reason to think that Mary could not be Queen of England – and a good one. Her own mother had been Queen of Castile in her own right, and such a remarkable one that the Pope of the day had written to her saying that if only he and she could have married and had a

of frendshepe. Alas ser, what hawe I offended yow, or what occasion of displeasure have I showed you, intending thus to put me from yow after this sorte I take God to my iudge. I haue bene to you a trwe and an humble wyfe evar confirmable to youre will and pleasure, that never contraried or gainesaide anye thynge there of, and beinge alwayes contented withe all thinges wheare in you had anye delight or daliaunce, whether it were litle or miche, withoute grudge or countenaunce of discontention or displeasure. I lowed for youre sake, all them whome ye loved, withar I had cause or no cawse, or whether they weare my frendes or enemies. I have bene yore wyfe these 20 yeres & moare, and ye haue had by me divers children, and when ye had me at the firste I take God too my Judge, that I was a very maide, and whither it be trwe or no, I put it to your conscience. Yf there be anie iust cause y ye can alledge againste me, either of dishonestie, or matter lawfull to put me from you, I am content to departe to my shame and rebuke. & if theire be none, then I praye you to let me have Iustice at youre handes: the kinge yo ffather was in his tyme of suche an excellent witt, that he was accovmpted amonge allmen for his wisdom, to be a second Solomon, And the kinge of Spaine my father ferdinando, who was reconed to be onne of the wisest Princes, y raigned in Spayne, many yeres before, who were bothe wyse men and noble Kinges: it is not therefore to be dowbted, but that they had gathered as wyze counsaylors vnto them of euery realme as to there Wysdomes they thowght mete. And as me semeth there weare in those dayes as wize and well serued in bothe the

Extract from a letter Katharine wrote to Henry when she heard that he was going to divorce her protesting that 'when ye had me at the first I take God too my Judge, that I was a very maide.'

son, that son would rule the world. Her own sister, Juana, having no brother living, had become Queen of Castile, and although she was so mad that in the end she had been kept under restraint, her right to be Queen had never been questioned. Ever since hope of a son had faded, Katharine had been training Mary to fit the rôle of Queen Regnant when the time came.

Henry felt very differently about leaving his throne to a daughter. If she married it must be to some great Prince and then England would become the appendage of some other power. And England's one experience of a woman on the throne had been unhappy. It had happened in the twelfth century and had resulted in a civil war of such savagery that people said Christ and all his Saints slept. Henry's concern about his country was

genuine enough and his fears were well founded. Two of his daughters
did reign over England: Mary married and made England an appendage
of Spain; Elizabeth by not marrying kept England free and by
statesmanship made it great, but her virginity meant the end of a dynasty.

Katharine's plea that her case should be judged in Rome was a sign that
she did not trust Wolsey – he was one of those who had decided that there
was some doubt about her marriage. Also by appealing to Rome, where
the wheels were known to turn very slowly, she was gaining time, time for
Henry to tire of Anne as he had tired of her sister and of Bessie Blount. She
would not have been human if she had not felt jealousy, even hatred, of the
new favourite and wished to place every obstacle in her way. It is
astounding that now that Anne was back at Court and Henry was
flaunting his infatuation so openly, Katharine through mannerliness and
iron self-control managed to behave to Anne just as she had in the old
days. If the records are true only once did she give even a hint that she
understood Anne's ambition and that was over a card game in which a good
deal depended upon drawing or turning up a king. Anne did so and
Katharine was heard to say, 'My Lady Anne, you have always the good hap
to stop at a king. But I think you are not like the others. You will have all or
nothing.' One can imagine their eyes meeting over the scattered cards.

Katharine's feelings about the whole matter were complicated by the
fact that she was still, and was always to remain, deeply in love with Henry
as a person. Later on, when he treated her badly, she never said a word
against him or allowed anyone else to do so in her presence. And when she
lay on her deathbed, she dictated a letter which ended, 'Lastly do I vow
that mine eyes desire you above all things.' Admittedly she signed it with a
last defiant 'Katharine the Queen' but that does not detract from the
sentiment. If Henry had been so completely detestable as he is often
shown to be, would a woman of Katharine's quality have loved him so
much and so long?

It was Henry's misfortune to be entangled with two of the most
stubborn women who ever existed.

Bronze Medal of Henry VIII

4

Campeggio's Mission

His Majesty has studied his case so diligently that I believe he knows more about it than any great theologian or jurist. He told me briefly that he wished nothing except a declaration whether his marriage was valid or not, always presuming it was not, and I think that an angel descending from heaven could not persuade him otherwise.

Cardinal Campeggio

Clement VII is a Pope chiefly remembered for the part he played – most unwillingly – in Henry of England's matrimonial tangle. He was naturally hesitant and timid, though half his blood was that of a family not remarkable for either characteristic – the Medici. He differed from them, too, in not being avaricious. He had a special reason for believing in the value of Papal Dispensations, for he was illegitimate by birth and it had taken a Dispensation to declare him legitimate and, therefore, eligible for election as Pope.

It could be said, with some truth, that he was the Pope responsible for the breach between the Church of England and the Church of Rome, but he lived in very troubled times, and the drama about to be played out in a misty little offshore island called England was overshadowed by what to any ordinary man must have seemed greater issues. The Ottoman Turks were threatening to overrun Christendom from the East and in Christendom itself there was bitter rivalry between the two Great Powers – the overgrown, polyglot Empire and France. England was not a Great Power at the time; in size, in population, in wealth and influence she was small, and until 1485 had been bleeding herself white in a Civil War which was not called by the pretty name – the Wars of the Roses – until two centuries later. And the Tudor dynasty was new. Henry VII had taken the Crown by force, but there were at least five men who had as good, or a better, claim. And Henry VII had been so busy putting down rebellions and restoring law and order that he had missed the chance of subsidizing

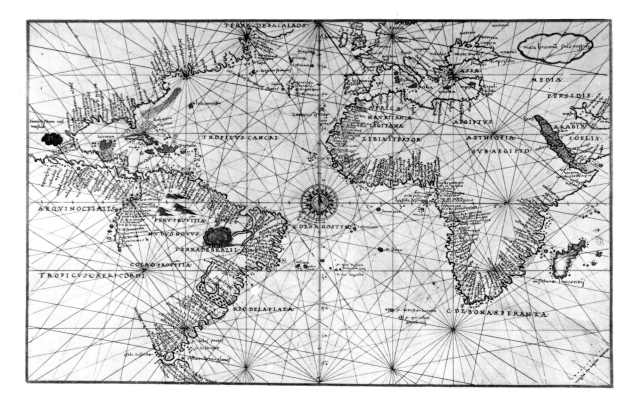

Christopher Columbus who, with three little ships, provided by Katharine of Aragon's mother, had set out to reach India from the West and stumbled upon the rich new world of the Americas.

Except as an ally, the last little weight in the balance of power, England was unimportant. And Clement, though in theory he ruled over all and was every lord's overlord, had little of the power that is derived from armies and navies. What were called the Papal States lay almost in the middle of the patchwork that was Italy while the rich alluvial States to the North and the sea bastion of Naples to the South were being contested for by Francis of France, and by the Emperor Charles.

Trying to keep a balance, siding now with one and then the other, Clement had done much to bring about his awkward position, with the *Landsknechts* – the best fighting men in the Empire, howling for Pope Luther under the very walls of the Castle of St Angelo – said to have been built by the Emperor Hadrian – who had also built the wall to protect Roman Britain from the pagan Picts and Scots, on that same negligible, offshore island. Now from England came requests for a decision which could not be reached without offending the Emperor, or by offending

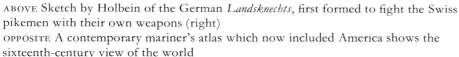

ABOVE Sketch by Holbein of the German *Landsknechts*, first formed to fight the Swiss pikemen with their own weapons (right)
OPPOSITE A contemporary mariner's atlas which now included America shows the sixteenth-century view of the world

Henry, drive him into the arms of France. There was also the problem of one Pope denying the validity of a Dispensation granted in good faith by his predecessor. A trying situation even for a strong and forceful Pontiff.

Clement's imprisonment was not very strict and soon, lightly disguised, he escaped. England, so soon to become at least in theory, an anti-Papist country, celebrated his escape joyfully, with all church bells ringing and bonfires in every village. By promising to pay a stiff ransom and to take firm action against the Lutherans in the north of Charles's Empire, Clement was soon on good terms with the Emperor and apparently in a position to decide between Henry and Katharine.

His crafty Medici blood showed in the way he dealt with the problem. He wrote agreeing to everything that Henry had demanded and then handed the document to one of his Cardinals, asking him to amend it. The Cardinal knew what the Pope wanted and amended it accordingly, omitting vital clauses, so that the decree was worthless. Clement was playing for time. So was Katharine. In pleading that the case should be tried in Rome, not in England, not by Wolsey, she would gain not only justice but delay.

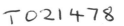

Painting by Holbein of ambassadors. Messages and letters between heads of state had to be delivered by hand

Henry was infuriated. Katharine continued to say 'No', she would not agree that she had never been his wife. Anne continued to say 'No', she would not bed with him until she was his wife. And the Pope's nonsensical answer was an insult to a man who took himself and his importance seriously. Would Clement have sent such an answer to the Emperor, or to Francis? Henry always had the happy knack of refusing to recognize what he wished to ignore, and he would not see that Wolsey's more subtle and diplomatic approach might have had a more pleasing result.

Wolsey had been to France – he had actually selected and dispatched his messengers to the Pope from there. Now he returned to England and, behaving correctly, rode straight to Richmond Palace where the Court was. He sent in to inquire where the King would wish him to go — meaning into which room for the private interview granted to every Ambassador back from an errand. Anne was with Henry and answered for him; 'Where else but here, where the King is?' It is often quoted as an example of her insolence, but it was more than that. It was a blow struck at Wolsey. When, weary from the journey and still in his riding-clothes, he entered the room and found Anne with Henry and saw that she was prepared to stay – and that Henry was prepared to allow her to stay during their private talk, he must have realized that this was no light passing fancy, as he had hoped. Katharine, daughter of a King, would never have taken such a liberty; no mere mistress would have been permitted to do so. All hope of seeing Henry marry the French Princess as soon as he was free, must have died then. Henceforth all his efforts to get what Henry wanted would be directed towards making Anne Boleyn, whom he had once called 'that foolish girl', Queen of England. Yet Wolsey loyally strove on and in the end was betrayed by everybody, even the master he had served so faithfully.

In Rome, Clement had thought of another delaying tactic and had found the ideal man to put it into action. The validity of Henry's marriage should be tried, not in Rome as Katharine had wished, but in England. Rome, however, would be represented by Cardinal Campeggio, given equal power with Wolsey. What other authority was conferred upon Campeggio was to be kept secret to the end.

Campeggio had been to England before and had, in the manner of the day, been given the title and the revenue of the Bishop of Salisbury. He might be said to understand the English as well as any Italian could do; but the main reason Clement had for sending him was that he could be trusted to be *slow*. He was ageing and he suffered from gout, now recognized as a form of arthritis which increases with age and can be exacerbated by physical strain and mental stress. Campeggio, so afflicted that sometimes he could not ride but had to take to a litter, sometimes so afflicted that he could not travel at all, took rather more than three months to make a journey which ordinarily took fifteen days.

And while he made his slow painful progress the Sweating Sickness broke out in England. It was a much-dreaded summer disease, only slightly less feared than the Plague. It may have been an extreme form of influenza; many of its victims died suddenly, and it was extremely contagious. Some people believed that it came in a wet summer, with the same kind of

Dr Butts, Henry VIII's physician whom Henry sent to attend Anne
when she was suffering from the Sweating Sickness

weather that produced murrain in cattle. It was said to select its victims
carefully, killing the young, the well fed and only those of English blood.
It was unknown on the Continent, except in Calais, where there were
many English people, since Calais was the last remnant of the Angevin
possessions in France.

Henry, like many other healthy, athletic men had a pathological horror
of illness. As soon as the Sweating Sickness struck, he went scurrying to
the country, moving from manor to manor.

Anne was already in the country, presumably safe. She had gone to
Hever to recover from some minor ailment – or as she sometimes did, to
show her displeasure with the way things were going, and to test the old

adage of absence making the heart grow fonder. There the Sweating Sickness caught up with her and both her father and brother fell ill, too.

Katharine, believing in the immunity granted her by her Spanish blood, and Wolsey, confident because he was old and had survived several epidemics, remained in London.

And with what joy must they both have heard of Anne's illness. The Hand of God? In their very different ways they were pious and had she died – without so far as either of them knew, having committed any mortal sin, they would have prayed for her soul.

Henry, informed of her later, more serious illness, did not go rushing to Hever. But he sent his own physician, Doctor Butts, to attend her – not that any physician had yet found a cure for the Sweat. And he wrote her a letter: 'There came to me suddenly in the night the most afflicting news that could arrive.' He went on to say that he would willingly bear half her malady if by doing so he could relieve her of pain. This could have been mere verbiage, but Henry, too, was pious after his fashion and would hardly have written such a God-challenging statement unless he meant it. For death was busy that summer. Move residence as often as he might, Henry always left some ailing, some dying, behind him. One of the dead was William Carey, Mary Boleyn's husband, Anne's brother-in-law. Never of much importance, though he owned some land, and had begotten an heir, William Carey dead made rather more impact than living he had done. His death made Henry show how fully he trusted Anne's judgment and ability to manage things.

Anne, her brother and her father all recovered from the Sweat; ignoring the two men, Henry gave Anne full charge of William Carey's estate, and of his son during his minority; she was even to arrange his marriage. This despite the fact that the Carey boy had a mother – once the King's mistress, a grandfather, and an uncle, both with more experience in administrating estates.

On his deathbed William Carey had sent a message to Wolsey asking him to favour the appointment of his sister, Eleanor Carey, as Abbess to Wilton Abbey. Never too busy to neglect a detail, Wolsey looked into the matter and discovered that Eleanor Carey, a professed nun, had borne two children, fathered by different priests, and also been another man's mistress. Wolsey himself had broken his vows of celibacy and kept a mistress, but that was in the past. Immorality in religious houses was one of the things which those who wished to reform the Church sharply criticized, so Wolsey thought it wise to forget any promise he might have made concerning Eleanor, and suggested instead the Prioress whom the nuns themselves favoured, saying that she was 'old, wise and discreet'. When younger, though, she had not lived an impeccable life. Anne chose to make of this appointment a test of strength with Wolsey, warmly supporting her relative by marriage and urging Henry to use his overriding authority. Henry, not wishing to offend the woman he loved, nor the man upon whom he still depended, appointed neither candidate, chose another woman and then wrote Anne a slavishly apologetic letter, explaining that he had tried to protect her conscience as well as his own.

The thing was, as Henry wrote to Wolsey, 'of no great matter', but it highlighted the laxity of behaviour in some religious houses, the part played by family influence where promotion was concerned, and Henry's dread of offending Anne. In the end the nuns seemed to have won the day; within a month or two the Prioress was Abbess of Wilton.

When Anne came back to London at the end of the summer, she was given an establishment of her own; a house in the Strand with a garden sloping down to the river. It belonged to Wolsey, and there is a suggestion that he offered it for her use. He may have hoped that given more privacy away from the Court over which Katharine still presided, Anne would allow herself to be seduced. Wolsey was worldly and wily and realized that her hold over Henry consisted largely of allowing him every intimacy except the ultimate one. And with Campeggio moving so slowly, there was still time for Henry to do rather more than kiss her breasts, and become disenchanted. It did not need Campeggio to explain to Wolsey that the Pope would look more favourably upon the annulment of the marriage if the outcome were to be the French marriage which would, in a devious way, show that Clement had French interests at heart.

Campeggio finally arrived in such a poor state – the gout had even affected his eyes – that the splendid reception which Wolsey had prepared for him fell flat. Campeggio just managed to reach a riverside house, outside London, and then next day, taking the easiest form of transport for a man in his condition – a barge on the river – he slid into London where Bath House had been put at his disposal, and there, for a fortnight, he lay suffering in a darkened room.

Wolsey visited him and learned with concern, but not – surely – with surprise that Campeggio wished to defer the trial as long as possible, and, in fact, to avoid it altogether. The King had doubts about his present marriage, but surely between them they could persuade him to accept Clement's offer to make it good.

Wolsey, who knew Henry and Anne, argued that this solution was impossible. Then, said Campeggio, other means must be tried, and, of course, the Pope must be informed and consulted at every turn. It would all take time.

As soon as Campeggio had partially recovered, he went, escorted by Wolsey, and again travelling by water, to be formally received by Henry and his Council, the peers, and all the Ambassadors in England, with one notable omission; it had been thought tactful not to invite the Spanish Ambassador, since the business which had brought Campeggio to England involved the possible downgrading of a Spanish Princess. Not that a word of business was spoken at this reception though it lasted four hours and was a great strain on Campeggio, who was at last allowed to go home and to bed.

Henry had thought it prudent to send Anne back to Hever – a useless precaution, since Campeggio knew all about her, and had indeed brought a message concerning her, direct from the Pope.

Next day, Henry, unable any longer to contain his impatience, went to call upon Campeggio who was still in bed, and whose first offer was calculated to enrage the King. The Pope, he said, was willing to grant another Dispensation to make good the marriage about which Henry's conscience was so troubled. This was the very last thing Henry desired and he embarked upon an argument, stating his own case so firmly that Campeggio reported that if an angel descended from Heaven he would not be able to persuade His Majesty.

Then Campeggio produced his second suggestion – far more to Henry's taste. All would be solved, he said, if only Katharine could be persuaded to enter a convent and take the veil.

There was a precedent for it. Louis XII's first wife, being childless, had gone into a convent, thus allowing him to marry and beget an heir. It was one way of ending a marriage without scandal and without much hurt to anyone. There were religious houses where a woman could live very comfortably; but, having taken the veil, she was regarded as dead to the world and her husband as a widower. This plan had the inestimable advantage of not bastardizing Mary.

Henry thought well of this suggestion; Katharine was extremely pious, well suited to the religious life. Her sexual life was over – he had indeed abandoned her bed long ago. What had she to lose? And so much to gain; her dignity, and his, would remain intact whereas the trial was bound to centre on intimate details – had she lost her maidenhead to Arthur or come virgin to Henry's bed?

He did not, however, face Katharine himself with this new proposition; he left that to Wolsey and Campeggio. They had underestimated Katharine's *real* piety which extended to the belief that anyone taking the veil should have a vocation. And she, she said, had none. She knew that her marriage was legal and she intended to live and die in the state of holy matrimony to which God had called her. The two Cardinals might go on their knees, beseeching her to change her mind; John Fisher, Bishop of Rochester, who agreed that her marriage had been legal, might advise her that this was an easy and rational way out of the deadlock; she was not to be moved. Later she made a private visit to Campeggio and in the most solemn manner swore that she had been a virgin when Henry married her, and if she were to be torn limb from limb for saying that she was his true wife, and should be born again to suffer the same fate for saying the same thing, she would say it. 'I am convinced she will act accordingly,' Campeggio wrote, resigning himself to the fact that there would be a trial, and that the whole sorry business would not be quickly and neatly dispatched. He had hoped to be back in Rome by Christmas; now he must winter in England, in a climate notoriously bad for gout.

It was over this rejection of the easy way out that Henry's attitude towards Katharine changed. Up to that point he had acted as the victim of his conscience, taking a sorry-for-all-this stance. Now he began to bring pressure to bear. When she asked whether Mary could come to Court to spend Christmas, he said, 'No', but if Katharine wanted to spend Christmas with Mary, who as Princess of Wales, had her own household, she was free to go. Katharine saw that as a retreat in the face of the enemy, leaving Anne Boleyn to preside over the riotous Twelve Days of Christmas.

Anne spent most of that autumn at Hever in a fever of impatience. Violent emotions are said to leave an imprint on the places where they have been felt; if that is so, it is understandable that her ghost, slightly too traditional to be very impressive, should drift across a lawn at Hever. She must have walked there amid the falling leaves waiting for news. Henry wrote and sent messages and doubtless she wrote to him, but of her letters so little remains. Women keep letters, re-read them, tie them into bundles with ribbon; men seldom do. Read and discard! Henry's letters to her – or some of them, were kept and eventually found their way into – of all places – the archives at the Vatican.

What would one not give, for instance, for some written evidence of how Anne felt about something that Henry did in November of that year.

He had always had a kind of extra sense, a finger on the pulse of public

One of Henry's love letters to Anne written while he was still married to Katharine of Aragon

opinion. Insulated as he was by courtiers and officials, he seemed to know what the people were saying, housewives' gossip, tavern talk. Most of it was completely uninformed and people believed that the King was seeking to get rid of good Queen Katharine in order to marry a Princess from France. Public sympathy was with Katharine, and Henry felt it necessary to redirect it back to himself. So he called a gathering in the Great Hall of Bridewell Palace.

There, to the Lord Mayor of London, the Aldermen, Sheriffs and other officials he made a thoroughly false-seeming speech. There are, however, *degrees* of falsity: it can partake of self-delusion; it can express, in lies, a deep, unadmitted truth. When Henry stood up on that Sunday afternoon and told the citizens about his troubled conscience, and spoke of the coming trial, saying that if it should declare his marriage good and legal, 'nothing could be more pleasant and acceptable to him', there may have been a grain of truth in it; subconsciously, he may have wished for a restoration of the old peaceful days before all this hubbub started. Any man, embarked on a voyage and faced with unexpected storms, might well wish that he were back on land and say that he wished for rescue. And

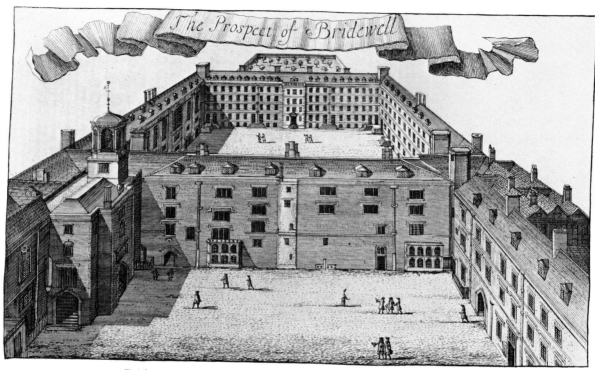

Bridewell Palace where Henry addressed the Lord Mayor of London, the Aldermen and other officials about his troubled conscience over his marriage to Katharine

when Henry went on to speak of Katharine – as he did – in fulsome terms of praise, he was not lying at all; she was in gentleness and all the qualities appertaining to nobleness of character 'without comparison'. It was not a downright lie to say that if he could marry again – *and the marriage be good* – he would choose her before all women. The qualifying clause saved it. The marriage had not been good because it had produced no heir to the throne.

Any man in the audience with property, a business, some hereditary office to bequeath, would have a fellow feeling for the King. And Henry – like his daughter Elizabeth – was a persuasive speaker. But Henry knew that in any body of men there was bound to be a few dissidents, so he ended his speech with a warning. One writer says it was an example of his characteristic brutality, but that is a judgment made with hindsight. So far Henry, in the context of his times, had been the reverse of brutal. Now he gave a hint that, if necessary, he could be: 'If I find anyone – whoever he is – who speaks in unsuitable terms of his prince, there is no head so fine but

I will make it fly.' Prophetic words. Several heads were to fly, but not yet. Henry still hoped for a legal, peaceful settlement.

Henry was well aware of Katharine's popularity — the pretty young Princess from Spain, dogged by ill-luck, widowed so soon and then remarried in a fairy-tale way. Unfortunate again in childbed. Time after time the people of England had wished her a happy delivery — and a son. They had shared her disappointments. And to the people of London she had a more realistic appeal, for soon after she became Queen, a May Day celebration had tipped over into a riot in which many apprentices, dissatisfied by their conditions, had taken part. The day was still remembered as Evil May Day, since so many were arrested and sentenced to be hanged; but Katharine had intervened on their behalf and Henry, to please her, had spared them. They were now grown men, with businesses and apprentices of their own; but they had not forgotten the good Queen who had begged for their lives, and even if they sympathized with Henry, they and their wives also hoped for a legal, peaceful settlement. Whenever Katharine appeared in public they were ready to shout, 'God save the Queen! God save Your Grace.' Henry noticed — or imagined — that she was showing herself more often than had been her habit, and asked her to restrict her outings. Since it was her boast that she obeyed the King in all things except those concerning God and her honour, she probably did as he requested.

The Cardinals who went about together as soon as Campeggio had partially recovered, had a very different reception in the London streets. Wolsey was respected and sometimes feared, but he was not loved; and Campeggio was regarded as the foreigner who had come to England for the specific purpose of getting rid of the good old Queen. The crowd was capable of showing hostility without saying a word or moving a finger and Campeggio, straight from Italy, was more sensitive than Wolsey. He made an attempt to get away from this unfriendly place, writing to Clement that he seriously considered that it would be better to have the case tried in Rome. To that letter there was no reply.

5

Wolsey's Defeat

An old man, broken with storms of state,
Is come to lay his weary bones among ye;
Give him a little earth for charity.

HENRY VIII: *Shakespeare*

Anne was back in London before Christmas. For one thing, as Henry was to prove again and again, he must have her with him. A day when he did not see her seemed as long as a fortnight. And the sense of nicety, or cunning, which had made it advisable to send her to Hever just as Campeggio arrived and was being received, had been wasted. The Pope knew, Campeggio knew, and more people every day were learning that if the King's marriage should be declared invalid, his new Queen would not be a French Princess but Anne Boleyn. Campeggio had told Wolsey and Wolsey had told Henry that the Pope was more likely to act positively on his behalf if he intended to marry somebody *other* than Mistress Boleyn.

Henry was intensely – and for once rightly – infuriated by this statement. He had started the whole procedure on a point of law, and had sought by legal means to obtain his freedom. It should have made no difference at all whom he wished to marry, once freedom was attained, or indeed if he intended to marry at all. The obvious injustice and veniality of the idea that things might have gone more easily had he intended to make a political marriage, rather than one for love, roused in him – as it would have done in most men – the spirit of 'I'll show you!'

He began to show them by bringing Anne back, not merely to her own house in London, but to Court. In whatever palace was being occupied at the time, Anne must have splendid apartments, next door to his own. The separate house smacked a little too much of the kept woman, the mistress. But the new arrangement had its embarrassments. There were now

OPPOSITE Like every young lady of good birth in the sixteenth century Anne was able to play the lute

Scene from a farce acted by a band of strolling players

virtually two Queens at Court: Katharine, anointed and crowned, and, until the Pope or his representative decided otherwise, indubitably Queen of England; and Anne, whom the King, in Campeggio's words, 'caresses openly and in public as if she were his wife. Notwithstanding this I do not think that he has proceeded to any ultimate conjunction. . . .'

It is possible that Henry hoped that by bringing Anne back to Court and making such display of affection, he would so affront Katharine that she would go away voluntarily. If so, he misunderstood her. Until she was ordered away, there she would be, by his side on all official occasions, a dumpy but dignified figure, wearing the jewels of the Queen of England. The people who wanted to be granted favours, or to draw the King's attention to themselves, or simply to be entertained, had, however, begun to desert Katharine and to frequent Anne's almost rival Court. Anne was adept at devising ways in which to divert Henry, particularly masques, the forerunners of plays, differing in that they were shorter and allowed women to participate. In the plays presented by the strolling players, and for years after proper theatres were established, no woman was allowed to take part, and women's roles were taken by slender young boys. In the private masque the ladies of the Court could display their charms, and Anne was a good actress.

Henry needed diversion; the autumn of 1528 had been a disappointment to him; he had imagined that Campeggio would come, decide in his favour and set him free to marry his love. That had not happened. Here was Campeggio in England and slowly, how slowly! making preparations for the trial to be held in England. And there were papers to be considered.

There was the original Papal Bull, giving permission for Henry to marry his brother's widow. It was in the Spanish archives and Charles had no intention of letting it out of his hands; but he had allowed copies to be made, attested copies, signed by lawyers. The man sent to bring back the document, but who had to wait while the copying was done, had been at least lukewarm in favour of Katharine's cause although he was one of her own chaplains. Brooding over the copy of the document, he was converted, and decided to write a book defending Katharine's marriage. Rapid publication was unknown when printing was still in its infancy and Thomas Abell's book was published just at the wrong time for him, when to write or speak against the legality of Henry's marriage to Anne was treason. Thomas Abell went to the Tower and was beheaded with other men more renowned; but he should be remembered for his courage.

There was, however, another paper, even more important than the original Papal Bull.

At the time when marriage between Katharine and Henry was being discussed the Spanish Ambassador had been a Doctor de Puebla. He had retired and gone back to Spain to die. When he did, his son, sorting through his papers, had come upon a paper, differing from the original Dispensation only in that it allowed Henry and Katharine to marry, *even if* her marriage to Arthur had been consummated. To Katharine who contended to the last that the marriage had never been consummated, this document was only important in that it strengthened her case. Even if she had been Arthur's wife in fact as well as in name, her marriage to Henry was still legal and good. She had a copy of that paper, and was careful not to let it out of her hands.

Campeggio also had a paper which Henry and Wolsey would dearly have loved to see. It contained his authorization from the Pope, power to hold the trial in England, to preside with Wolsey, and if possible give a verdict with which his fellow Cardinal concurred. But what else did it say? Why was he so secretive about it? No paid spy, no bribed servant ever caught a glimpse of it. In the autumn of the next year when Campeggio was at last leaving for Rome, despite the fact that he was Papal Legate and thus traditionally free from such procedure, his luggage was most thoroughly ransacked at Dover. The document was not found; Campeggio had destroyed it.

This prolonged waiting time bore hard on everyone concerned. Katharine endured it with a semblance of serenity; she knew that she was right; she still hoped that Clement might change his mind and decide either that no trial was needed, or, if needed, that it should be held in Rome as she had from the first begged him to do. Except that she was not allowed to see her daughter she was suffering no positive deprivation. Henry suffered far more, eager to marry Anne, to beget the boy he was sure she would give him. Yet he still wished for everything to be done legally and properly; and he was still under pressure from Anne who, unless she were indeed a witch and certain of her future, must have suffered the most, since her position was utterly insecure, completely dependent upon Henry's favour. She must have gone to bed every night unsure of what the next day would bring. If it brought a change in Henry, she would, unlike Katharine, have no friend either in England or on the Continent. She had not even the consolation of knowing that her chastity was recognized, except by Wolsey who deplored it, and by Campeggio who viewed it dispassionately. The Spanish Ambassador, Chapuys, referred to her as 'The Concubine'; less polite people called her a 'goggle-eyed whore'.

What she said to Henry, and what he said to her, when the masques, the music-making and the dances were over, nobody now can know. (There was once a theory that everything done or said on this small earth, to its inhabitants the centre of the Universe, could be seen and heard if only the observer could get far enough away; everything was recorded in outer space. Some portion of outer space has now been explored, but so far nothing to support that theory has been uncovered. So we are left with imagination.)

Little imagination is needed to understand why that year, Henry

OPPOSITE Anne Boleyn as St Barbara. Women could not take part in public performances of plays but in private, the ladies of the Court performed in masques and Anne was a good actress

As Wolsey's fall became imminent, Henry VIII was moving towards the break with
Rome which would result not only in Wolsey's banishment from Court but in the
execution of Sir Thomas More and Cardinal Fisher

allowed Anne to take upon herself one of the prerogatives of the Queens of England – the preparation and sending out of the cramp rings.

There was a myth that the King of England could, by a touch, cure the complaint known as 'scrofula', a visible form of tuberculosis which showed itself in swollen glands and skin lesions. In a similar way, Queens of England were believed to be able to give a gold or silver ring the power to fend off night-cramp – horrible enough to this day, but in the past endowed with a special horror, since it was thought to come straight from the Devil. The rings were placed in a bowl, prayers were said and blessings invoked, then the Queen took each one and rubbed it between her palms. Recipients of such rings valued them highly and passed them on as heirlooms. Both Henry and Anne must have known very well that the mystical preventive could not work through the medium of hands which had *not* been anointed with holy oil in the Coronation ceremony. Yet Henry, perhaps as part of the defiance which was mounting in him, perhaps as a placatory gesture to Anne, even perhaps as another subtle insult to Katharine, allowed Anne to send out the cramp rings quite openly, and to important people. Whatever the motive, the message was clear; Henry regarded Anne as Queen already, and was sticking to his intention to make her so in fact at the first possible opportunity.

The first possible opportunity! So long in coming. It was July, high, hot summer, before Campeggio was ready to sit in judgment – with Wolsey – in the Great Hall of the Monastery of the Blackfriars. Some of the delay was due to the Pope being ill – at one point so ill that his death was reported, but as Mark Twain said when he was reported to be dead, the rumour was greatly exaggerated. In July 1529 Clement was alive and well and capable of refusing Campeggio's pathetic suggestion that he should take, at the trial, second place to Wolsey. By this time Campeggio had seen Henry, seen Katharine, seen Anne and had shrunk away from the prospect of being the point at which three such exceptionally stubborn people would collide. Clement refused Campeggio's request, and all that remained for the Legate was to go ahead with the trial and then, as a last resort, fall back upon his secret orders.

Once again, Anne was at Hever. It may have been from that same sense of nicety which had sent her there in the previous autumn when Campeggio arrived. It may have been that Henry thought Hever a safer and definitely more healthy place than London in midsummer; or it may have been that she herself had chosen a temporary retirement, strengthening her hold, letting Henry learn how well – or how badly – he could get on without her during what was bound to be a very trying time for him. One must feel that a more ordinary – or a weaker – woman would have wished to be there on the spot, to hear, at first hand, what had been said at the court, to rejoice with Henry if things seemed to be going right, comfort him if they went otherwise. But Anne was neither ordinary nor weak. And it is safe to say that for Henry as a man – which, under all the trappings of Royal splendour, he was – she had little feeling at all.

So she went to Hever with its green lawns and shady trees and Henry, for once braving out summer in London, where if there was not an epidemic of Plague or Sweating Sickness, there were the putrid summer fevers, the stinking streets, the conduits which served both as water-supply and sewer, sources of infection, duly presented himself at the Blackfriars court when the usher called, 'Henry, King of England, come into the court.' Katharine, called in similar terms, came too, but she did not take the seat allotted to her. She ignored Wolsey and Campeggio and all the assembled peers of England, went straight to Henry, knelt and said something – in all innocence – which Henry remembered long after he had dismissed from his mind all her appeals to his sentiment. 'I beseech you for all the love that hath been between us, let me have justice and right, take of me some pity and compassion for I am a poor woman, and a stranger, born out of your dominion. I have here no assured friend and much less indifferent counsel. I flee to you, *as the head of justice within this realm.*'

She, a woman of the utmost piety, said those words in the presence of two men upon whom the Pope had bestowed the rank of Cardinal, whom the Pope had appointed to judge the case, and one of whom had come from Rome as Papal Legate, His Holiness's direct representative.

She went on to remind Henry of how good a wife she had been, how many children she had borne him, and how he must know that she was virgin when he married her. All very embarrassing! Henry said nothing, he sat staring straight ahead until, knowing that she had failed, Katharine rose from her knees and walked out, making no appeal to the Cardinals. The action emphasized her words; Henry was the head of justice within this realm.

The seed was planted; it took time to reach full growth, but it grew.

The so-called 'trial' dragged on, Wolsey and Campeggio, all the learned churchmen and the peers of England listening to long-drawn-out arguments about the sexual potency of a boy of Arthur's age and whether the bed-sheets had born evidence of a broken hymen when Katharine was Arthur's bride or Henry's. Finally at the end of it all Campeggio announced – and surely with the greatest relief – that this was virtually a Roman court, and all Roman courts took a long summer vacation; so this court was closed until October, and when it reopened it would be, not in London but in Rome.

That summer's Progress must have been a curious one. The Progress was a kind of annual holiday when the monarch went out of London to visit his own manors or those of some particularly favoured lord who would provide, sometimes at ruinous cost, accommodation and entertainment for the whole Court. Progresses also gave ordinary people a chance to see their King and there may be some significance in the fact that when, years afterwards, a rebellion against Henry was mounted, it was in the North, in areas where he had never been seen, so handsome, so kingly and so gifted with that inexplicable thing called 'charm'.

Katharine went with Henry on the Summer Progress of 1529; she was still Queen of England and would be until in faraway Rome at some date not yet fixed, she was declared to be otherwise. But Anne went, too, rather more confident than ever. On pompous occasions Katharine stood there, Queen of England, gracious and dignified. But she no longer cared for riding and hunting, pursuits which Anne shared with Henry. And in the evenings, when there was nothing else to do, Anne and Henry could talk about the future they were to share, the children they would have, children who, as she insisted, must be both Royal and legitimate. And they could castigate Wolsey.

Anne, although she had responded to Wolsey's pretended friendship with gifts, with a letter or two, still regarded him as her enemy and Henry was inclined to blame the whole fiasco of the Blackfriars trial upon his Chief Minister who had always seemed to be omniscient and omnipotent. Wolsey was now about to pay the price of seeming to be all-powerful and having failed on a crucial issue. Henry had given Wolsey no chance to explain or to excuse himself. He had come on this awkward, triangular Progress and left Wolsey to wind up the disastrously futile Blackfriars court and then to bring Campeggio to take formal leave.

Both Henry and Anne were also incensed by Katharine's behaviour at Blackfriars; they felt – with some justice – that in refusing the jurisdiction of the court, refusing even to sit through its sessions, she had contributed to the failure of the whole thing, of which they had had such hopes. And she had gained her point; she had always wished the matter to be discussed and decided in Rome, and now it was to be, after more intolerable delay. Henry now ceased to keep up the pretence of being on friendly terms with

her, abandoned the good-brother-and-sister relationship and hardly saw her except on public occasions.

So, in September they all came to a country manor-house called Grafton, near to Stony Stratford in Northamptonshire. It was sizeable as most manor-houses were, but not large enough to accommodate the King, his attendants, the Queen and her ladies, and Anne and her ladies, who now outnumbered Katharine's. Some courtiers had to find lodgings in other houses. It was probably this overspill problem which suggested to Anne a malicious way of shaming Wolsey, and at the same time ensuring that Henry saw as little of him as possible. Steadfast as Henry had stayed in his attachment to her, undeterred by delays and difficulties, she knew that his moods veered easily and she was afraid that, faced with the man who had grown old in his service, his heart would soften.

So, when the two Cardinals rode their mules into the courtyard at Grafton, just before midday dinner, Campeggio was welcomed – not by Henry, but by the proper official, and led away to the apartment prepared for him. For Wolsey there was no welcome, and no room. Henry was still

OPPOSITE Hunting was one of the entertainments presented for the King's pleasure on the Royal Progresses. 'Le depart pour la chasse', an early sixteenth-century French tapestry
BELOW Cushion cover in white satin and coloured silks depicting hunting scenes

in his anti-Wolsey mood, and although he was in the house, did not go out. Almost certainly Anne must have looked from a window and watched this final humiliation of her old enemy. She expected him to turn his mule and ride away.

East Anglian herself, she should have known better; shamed, deserted by all but a real friend or two, an object of derision, Wolsey sat on his mule, prepared so to sit until the animal dropped under him. He was sure that if only he could meet Henry face to face and explain, all would be well, so he waited. And presently Sir Henry Norris, Henry's friend, his Groom of the Stole, one of whose duties was to sweep a sword under the King's bed and behind any wall-hanging which might conceal an assassin, ran out and offered Wolsey his own room, where he could wash and change.

Wolsey was now under the roof at Grafton and thus entitled to take dinner in the Great Hall. He went down and men who had fawned upon him while his power was undisputed, turned away. The King, although he did not intend to dine in the hall, was there, ready to take leave of Campeggio which he did in the briefest, most formal terms. The two Cardinals knelt before him, but it was Wolsey whom Henry helped to his feet, and putting an arm round his shoulders, led him off to the embrasure of a large window for the private, or semi-private talk which Anne had feared.

Henry began on an almost apologetic note; he said that he had not seen Wolsey since the Blackfriars court because the result had so maddened him that he could not bear to see anybody who had had anything to do with it. And Wolsey, that skilled diplomat, then explained that he could perhaps have kept the court in session, could perhaps even have forced through a verdict in Henry's favour; *but* such a verdict would not have been accepted by Rome and if on the strength of it Henry had married Mistress Boleyn, it would have been a bigamous marriage, more open to question than his present one.

Henry seemed to accept this argument. He excused himself, saying that he had promised to dine with Mistress Boleyn, but that he would talk to Wolsey after dinner. Wolsey sat down to eat with better appetite than he had enjoyed for some weeks, and everybody treated him with the respect which had been so sadly lacking about an hour earlier. Even those who hated him regarded him as reinstated.

Dinner with Anne must have been less enjoyable. We have only the word of those who waited at table to go upon, but it sounds authentic enough. The prospect of a reconciliation between Henry and Wolsey frightened her, and as usual with people of her nature, fear made her

Hever Castle, the Boleyn family home, was bought by Anne's great grandfather, Sir Geoffrey Boleyn, in the fifteenth century

aggressive. She scolded Henry for dealing so gently with her enemy – and his. She reminded Henry how tricky and cunning, how much involved with Campeggio and the Pope Wolsey was. She showed her anger and disgust 'as far as she durst'. And that was very far indeed. Somebody who did not much approve of her said that she was as brave as a lion; and at that moment it must have seemed to her that she had little to lose. Henry had promised to marry her, and after all this time was as far from being able to do so as he had been when the promise was made. Wolsey, restored to favour would be working against her; the case, presently to be tried in Rome would almost certainly be decided in Katharine's favour and Mistress Boleyn would remain Mistress Boleyn, with some slight material gain, sufficient jewels to sell and keep her in moderate comfort – but with her name irrevocably blackened.

Those close to the King knew the truth, she had never been Henry's mistress; people outside the Court, outside the country, found difficulty in believing this and scandalous tales abounded. Old stories of Mary

Boleyn's light behaviour in France were disinterred and told as concerned with Anne, even the gossip about Anne's mother was remembered. When Henry displeased her, she could always remind him of what her association with him had already cost her in reputation, and she would hardly have been human if she did not follow it with the suggestion that it had better end, here and now. She could go back to Hever. Enter a

An illustration from *The Booke of Hunting* entitled 'Of the place where and howe an assembly should be made, in the presence of a Prince or some honorable person'

convent. Such a thought was so intolerable to Henry that he was ready with apologies, with promises. Then, for she too was a creature of moods, she would relent and be charming, thinking up some new diversion for his pleasure.

What happened at Grafton that day was a typical example. Henry kept his promise to talk with Wolsey later and that conversation was held in more privacy than the embrasure of a window afforded. Henry could not then have made plain to his old Minister that this was only a temporary reconciliation, for Wolsey went cheerfully away to a lodging one of his servants had found for him, understanding that the talk was to be resumed in the morning.

He rose early – his lodging was three miles from Grafton – and arrived to find Henry and Anne, some chosen attendants, all young and gay, already mounted and about to set out to visit a new deer-park at Hartwell where they would eat a very informal dinner out of doors – a picnic, though the word was not then in use. There was time only for the most cursory leave-taking; and this time, as Wolsey rode away, with Campeggio for company, he knew the worst. The failure at Blackfriars combined with Anne's influence, had ended his career. (Yet, curiously, he still felt that if he could only meet his King again, face to face, all might be mended. Anne's cousin, Catherine Howard, thirteen years later, condemned to die, was equally sure that she had only to *see* Henry and her life would be spared. She tried to waylay him on his way to chapel in Hampton Court, and her ghost is said to haunt the gallery where she tried, and failed. Both the old, infinitely experienced statesman and the frivolous young girl-Queen had recognized the soft, weak streak in Henry. He could be brutal, give brutal orders, but he could not bear to face his victims, or to watch the orders being carried out. The epithet 'sadistic', sometimes applied to him, is misplaced. His temper was already souring and was, with the years, to become savage, but he never enjoyed seeing people suffer.)

Wolsey, defeated, rode away on that September morning and never saw Henry again.

6

Waiting, Waiting...

Mademoiselle Boleyn has come to the court at London and the King has set her in a very fine lodging, which he has furnished very near his own. Greater court is paid to her every day than has been for a long time paid to the Queen.

Cardinal du Bellay

Wolsey's chief secular office had been that of Chancellor; he did not resign. Henry sent the Dukes of Norfolk and Suffolk to ask him to hand over the Great Seal of England, and Wolsey refused, questioning their authority. Henry sent a written, signed order; the seal was handed over and given to Sir Thomas More.

The choice was significant. More was not a churchman, he was a lawyer and a dead honest one. And with the rarest of exceptions the Chancellor of England had always been an ecclesiastic – a custom dating back to a time when only churchmen were literate. That Henry should appoint More is indicative of a change of mind, of mental climate, of the so-called 'Reformation' for which Anne is often solely blamed. And wrongly. The feeling that Holy Church exacted too much, owned too much and often did too little to justify such exactions, had been growing for a long time, not only in England, but in Europe too. Good pious Catholics who would never miss Mass on Sunday, or ignore a feast-day, or a fast, resented paying such a tax as the so-called 'Peter's Pence'; a penny a year on every hearth if there were more than one in a household. At a time when a cow could be bought for fourpence, and there was a building boom, every new room with its hearth, this was not a popular tax. Nor was the one which took from every new incumbent, be it to a diocese or a humble country parish, his first year's stipend. There were even pettier things; the cloth in

OPPOSITE Thomas Cranmer who, as an obscure cleric, suggested that Henry should canvas the opinion of the universities in Britain and abroad as to the validity of Henry's marriage to Katharine

which a corpse was wrapped before it was coffined automatically became the property of the priest who conducted the funeral. And many monks and nuns lived – like Eleanor Carey – scandalous lives. The need for reform was recognized, and perhaps Henry in choosing a layman to hold an office that had virtually become a perquisite of the Church was moving in step with the times.

About the legality of Henry's marriage to Katharine, More had so far expressed no opinion. It was a matter for the law to decide, but he accepted his new office on condition that he should be allowed liberty of conscience. Henry agreed. The two were good friends, enjoying each other's company and conversation, and neither man could possibly have visualized in the autumn of 1529, the tragic end which More's conscience would force upon him within less than four years.

Disappointing as the year 1529 had been to the man eager to possess his beloved and beget – God willing – a son, and to the woman who would have the Crown or nothing, it brought some compensations; they had Wolsey's wealth and his many properties to play with. An exceedingly ancient law called *praemunire* which made it an offence for any English subject to communicate with the Pope without first consulting his King, had been brought out, dusted off and applied to Wolsey. He was tried and found guilty, and although he had been pardoned, all his property was forfeit to the Crown. Henry could take possession of Hampton Court, The More and half a dozen other manors, but he had no right at all to York House which was in Westminster and which Wolsey had occupied because he was Archbishop of York – a place he had never seen.

Henry took it, however, and there were no protests. Anne had lived at Court, occupied for a brief time a loaned house, returned to Court, and was now to have her own palace. Wolsey, like many ambitious, self-made men, was a great builder, and had spent money on enlarging and embellishing York House; but it was not good enough for Anne. It stood in a heavily built-up area and had no grounds – this at a time when any house of substance in the city had a garden, often an orchard.

Anne must have not merely a garden but a deer-park; so the area must be cleared, humble people sent to live elsewhere. It is said that these displaced people received no compensation. That statement is open to question. Neither Henry nor Anne was mean by nature and both were greedy for popularity. The people whose houses had been demolished probably received gifts not mentioned in the records. Londoners, even humble ones, were not the meekest of people and the idea that they would

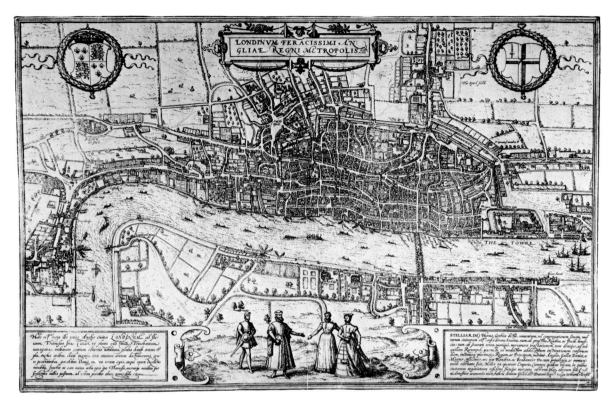

Map of London in the mid-sixteenth century attributed to Georg Hofnagel

vacate their homes and go away uncompensated is hardly conceivable.

The great advantage of the new palace, which was to be called Whitehall, was that in it there would be no accommodation for Katharine who was grimly holding on to her position, occupying the Queen's apartments in all the older palaces, Greenwich being her favourite. (Years later and entirely to please himself, Henry was to build another palace, rightly called Nonsuch, a place of fabulous beauty, forestalling Versailles; and that short-lived glory may have owed something to lessons learned during the modification and reconstruction of Whitehall.)

Alongside the shared interest of planning and building, Henry and Anne could now cherish a hope of a solution to their intractable problem. It came from an unlikely source – an obscure man, a scholar, a cleric without a living, acting as tutor to two boys in a house at Waltham. Two of Henry's friends stayed there and at the dinner-table the question of the

ABOVE Nonsuch Palace, plans for which may have owed much to Anne and Henry's designs for Whitehall

RIGHT *Great Harry* which carried 349 soldiers, 301 mariners and 50 gunners. Henry's expansion of the navy made England a much more powerful force in Europe

marriage was brought up. Thomas Cranmer said that he had not studied the matter closely, but if he were in the King's position, he would canvass the opinion of all the universities, not merely in England, but on the Continent. If a majority of scholars, learned in law and theology, could ponder the matter and decide in Henry's favour, the impending trial in Rome would be either unnecessary, or a mere formality.

Henry seized on this suggestion with avidity; 'He has the right sow by the ear!' he exclaimed. Messengers were dispatched to the universities, and Cranmer was brought to London and set on the lower rung of the ladder that was to lead to the Archbishopric of Canterbury – and then to death at the stake. And, since the opinion of wise men was being sought, why should not Jewish scholars be consulted? They of all people should be able to interpret the conflicting texts of Leviticus and Deuteronomy. The Jews had been banished from England two hundred and forty years earlier; Katharine's mother, Isabella, had driven them from Spain, but in

other countries they had survived, little close-knit communities, under-privileged minorities, now being asked to explain Mosaic law for the benefit or the detriment of a Christian, Catholic King.

When it began, this canvass of scholars had a predictable result. All the Lutheran-orientated countries in the North of Europe would certainly seize on any opportunity to go against Papal authority; Italy and Spain and the Southern part of the Empire could almost as certainly be counted upon to say that Julius's Dispensation was good. France was a possible marginal case, not because France was not Catholic – it was, but Francis and Charles were still at odds and England, as ally or enemy, was of increasing importance to France. Henry VIII was reviving the Navy which his father – concerned with so many domestic affairs – had allowed to rot. Henry VIII had inherited seven ships; he had added twenty-four, including the *Great Harry* which was furnished with guns. And although the English yeoman-archers with their longbows, so successful at Crécy and Agincourt, were now a little outdated by the introduction of artillery, they were not to be discounted. They could discharge several deadly flights of arrows while the more modern guns were being reloaded. So when the University of Paris presently returned an opinion likely to be displeasing to Henry, Francis brought pressure to bear until it was reversed. Padua, in Italy, most unexpectedly, concluded that the marriage was not legal.

Words, words and more waiting.

By far the easiest and simplest solution would have been for Katharine to die and it is safe to say that in almost any other country she would have been poisoned. In Italy, poisoning had become a fine art; one of Clement's predecessors, a Borgia Pope, claimed to have got rid of an enemy by a poison so subtle that it took months to take effect. Not only food and wine could be lethal, there were ways of impregnating articles of clothing, or even letters. In France, too, poisonings were frequent and in Spain two

Battle of the Spurs, thought to have been painted for Henry VIII, shows the English cavalry routing the French forces in 1513

heirs to the throne had died suddenly and in mysterious circumstances.

For some reason poisoning had never become a habit in England; both Edward II and Richard II had been unwanted, deposed and murdered, but not by poison, though Edward II was killed in such a peculiarly brutal manner that a fatal dose would have seemed merciful. King John, greatly hated, had died in 1216 from what may have been poisoning, but there was a counter-claim, gluttony – a surfeit of peaches and new cider had brought about his end.

Witches and deadly brews have always been closely associated and if Anne were indeed a witch, it seems strange that she did not make some attempt, at least, to remove Katharine by such means, and at a time when the Queen's death would have served her purpose. Seven years later, when Katharine died of what modern medicine thinks was cancer, Anne was accused of poisoning her, but by then it was greatly to Anne's advantage to have Katharine alive and well.

There was, during this waiting time, one case of poisoning, for which it was whispered Anne was to blame. In Bishop Fisher's house a white powder was dropped into some porridge – or broth – and several of his servants, and some beggars who had devoured what was left of the dish, died. Fisher, perhaps because he ate sparingly, was only indisposed. But to kill Fisher merely because he sided with Katharine and leave Katharine, the real obstacle, untouched would have been the action of a stupid woman, and that Anne was not. (Fisher's cook was accused of being the tool of either Anne or her father, and condemned to death by being boiled, a sentence which was carried out. Cooks were supposed to taste every dish before it went to table, but food passed through many hands, sometimes travelled considerable distances between kitchen and table, and it was prepared, served and indeed eaten in appallingly unhygienic conditions. The Bishop's household may have simply suffered from a virulent food-poisoning such as botulism.)

It may be relevant to remark that when, later on, Katharine and Mary were told to be careful of what they ate and drank, the warning was issued by a foreigner, Chapuys, the Emperor's Ambassador who came to England in 1529, who adopted Katharine's cause and was, therefore, completely anti-Anne. Chapuys was a great letter-writer and he kept his master well informed with fact, with gossip. He had reliable contacts, he had spies, but he did not scorn relaying things told him by 'a certain gentleman'. Many of his letters survive; where Katharine was concerned

Sixteenth-century drum-type watch of gilt bronze

Although Wolsey had fallen from favour, Henry still sent his physician, Dr Butts, to
attend him when Wolsey became unwell

he was to prove himself a sturdy, courageous friend, but he was biased
against Anne and since his reports are such a mine of information and
much used, he has rather distorted posterity's view of her. It was he who
first referred to her as 'The Concubine'.

The Blackfriars court having referred the case to Rome, Clement was
within his rights to invite – or order – Henry to attend a new trial there;
and Henry was within his rights in refusing to go. There was another old
rule, as moss-grown as the *praemunire* brought into action against Wolsey;
ne extra Angliam litigare cogantur. No Englishman could be tried in a
foreign court.

This refusal to go to Rome and be tried meant further delay – welcome
to Clement, most unwelcome to Henry, and containing just a hint of
something which perhaps neither man recognized immediately; the
possibility of a break away from Papal authority because the English were
different – a law unto themselves. The English had been one of the last
peoples to be completely brought into the Christian fold, missionaries and
the early Bishops had not found things easy and more than once there had
been head-on collisions between English Kings and the Papacy. On one
occasion because the Pope would not accept a King's choice of

Archbishop of Canterbury, and the King would not accept the Pope's, the See stood vacant for years: and the quarrel which ended in the murder of Thomas à Becket was fundamentally a struggle for power between Church and State.

For Clement, every day's delay was a day gained – anything might happen; Henry might tire of Anne; Katharine might die; the Emperor might decide to support his aunt with more than a few polite gestures. For Henry every day's delay was a day wasted, and for Anne a prolongation of nerve-racking suspense, concealed by half-hysterical gaiety. In addition to everything else she was concerned about Henry's ambivalent attitude towards Wolsey.

Wolsey had wintered in Esher, a place which did not suit his health. He fell ill, and Henry sent to him that same physician – Doctor Butts – who had gone to attend Anne when she was suffering from the Sweating Sickness. Doctor Butts, who must have been an enlightened man, reported that what Wolsey really ailed was a broken spirit due to the withdrawal of the King's favour. Henry straightway sent a gift and a heartening message – and persuaded Anne to do the same. But he did not recall his old favourite, or reinstate him. He allowed him to go to his long-neglected diocese of York. And there Wolsey seemed to undergo a great change, abandoning all pomp and splendour, living very simply and attending to his ecclesiastical duties with assiduity.

It should have been a case of out of sight, out of mind, but Henry missed Wolsey. Missions to the Continent which the old statesman would have conducted skilfully and with some chance of success, were bungled, noticeably by Anne's father and brother; and at home, Thomas Cromwell who had stepped into Wolsey's place – except for the Chancellorship – and who was anxious to please the King in every possible way, was less congenial as a person. Wolsey and Cromwell came from much the same lower-middle-class background, but Wolsey had outgrown his in a way that Cromwell never did.

In Wolsey, ambition still simmered behind the posture of humility and the wearing of a hair shirt. He made the fatal mistake of trying to intrigue his way back to power, for though he had virulent enemies in the Boleyn party at Court, he also had friends. His activites were discovered, the old charge of offending against *praemunire* was revived and Wolsey was recalled to London to face trial and certain death for treason. By a singular irony – a coincidence that no fiction writer dare invent – the man sent to arrest him and escort him to London was Harry Percy, that wilful boy, now Earl of Northumberland.

92

Sir Thomas Wyatt. He was a cousin of Anne's
and although accused of having been her lover,
he seems to have admired her only from afar
within the conventions of courtly love

They got no farther south than Leicester and there age, physical frailty
and mental distress combined to deal the death-blow. Stumbling into
Leicester Abbey, Wolsey said, 'Father Abbot, I have come to lay my bones
amongst you.' On his deathbed he murmured, 'If I had served God as
diligently as I have done my King, He would not have given me over in
my grey hairs.'

That threat made long ago by an angry, impotent girl had been
effective; both directly and indirectly, that silly girl had brought about the
fall of the greatest man of his generation.

The King of France sent Henry not only messages of sympathy in his
dilemma, but advice. Marry Anne and let the Pope and the Emperor do
what they liked. This was not quite disinterested advice; the least harm it
could do to Henry would be to set the Pope and the Emperor against him,
leaving him no friend on the Continent except France. The most it could
do would be to provoke Clement into excommunicating Henry, and for a
monarch excommunication was a very serious thing indeed. It cancelled
all vows of allegiance ever made to him and gave any other monarch leave
to invade and take his kingdom – if he could.

Fortunately for Henry, and for England, Henry's Council, when he consulted its members about Francis's advice, was overwhelmingly opposed to it. Only two members, Anne's father and her uncle, the Duke of Norfolk, voted in favour. And neither Henry nor Anne was yet quite desperate enough to act precipitately and plunge into a marriage which might, in its turn, be of questionable validity. Better wait!

All the time, Anne's enemies were busy. Henry Percy's wife complained – probably with every justification – that he was not behaving to her as a husband should. He retorted that he was *not* her husband, having been previously contracted to marry Anne Boleyn. This angry marital exchange was promptly reported to Henry. He ignored it at the time, but remembered it later. Then Charles Brandon, Duke of Suffolk, saw fit to tell Henry that Anne had been Thomas Wyatt's mistress.

Thomas Wyatt was one of Anne's many cousins, and out of the obscurity that blurs her earlier years there is a hint that they may have spent some of their childhood together. Then their ways had separated, she had gone to France and he had gone to Cambridge. They met again at Court when she returned from France. Although only nineteen, he was already married, but he fell in love with her in the stylized, almost asexual way fashionable in Court circles. Adoration from afar: love-poems; flattering speeches; elation at a smile; despair at a frown. One of his verses expresses how exactly he understood the situation – and Anne herself.

> And graven with diamonds in letters plain
> There is written her fair neck around,
> *Noli me tangere*, for Caesar's I am
> And wild for to hold, though I seem tame.

Anne denied that there had ever been more than friendship between her and Wyatt and Henry found it easy to believe. On her return to Court from France it was Harry Percy who had attracted her attention, and her hopes; then she had set her heart on the Crown. Nor was she the woman to be seduced by fair speeches and languishing looks – as he knew to his cost. He dismissed all the rumours lightly.

We have hearsay talk about bursts of temper in which Anne could reduce the big, blustering King of England to tears. Almost certainly some of these were occasioned by Katharine's continued presence at Court and her continuing to take her place as Queen on all official occasions. But when Henry did put an end to this phase it was not only because of Anne's nagging; some of his friends had pointed out that it would be more in keeping with his talk about his conscience if he broke off all relationship with Katharine. If his conscience told him that she was not his wife, then she was not Queen, so why did she always appear on State occasions? Why did she accompany him on the Summer Progresses?

In the summer of 1531, this custom was broken. The whole Court went to Windsor and there Katharine was left while Anne continued the Progress with Henry and certain favoured courtiers. Some people believe that her mother was taken along as chaperone – and that would be in accordance with the desire to have everything done correctly and conventionally; others hold that Anne went alone, the only woman in a male party – and that would be in accordance with her known preference for male company. She seems to have lacked the ability to form firm friendships with women – the exception being Thomas Wyatt's sister, Lady Lee, who was faithful to the bitter end. Historically it is a pity because women write letters and cherish memories and keepsakes.

Henry, in typical fashion, rode away without telling Katharine that this was the end of all pretence. She may have guessed, but she had always said that she would stay at Court until told to leave; so she waited, and presently the message came. When Henry returned to London he did not wish to find her there; she was to take up residence at The More.

The More was one of the houses formerly belonging to Wolsey, large enough and comfortable enough for him to have entertained the King and Queen there in times past. It was near Harrow-on-the-Hill, so within easy reach of London; friends and Ambassadors could visit her, though the ban on Mary remained.

Anne was delighted by Katharine's banishment, but her pleasure was mitigated when accounts came in of how, all along the streets and roads, people crowded to cheer Katharine and wish her well. It was obvious now, even to the slowest-witted, that the King was getting rid of the good old Queen, and intended to replace her by Nan Bullen – the coarsened version of Anne's name.

That summer, in the country-houses which Henry honoured by accepting their hospitality – and Henry had probably chosen them with care – Anne was treated as Queen-to-be, and enjoyed the relaxed atmosphere, the hunting and the gambling. Then she came back to London and the crowds were sullen and silent and now and again a voice shouted, from safe anonymity, 'We want no Nan Bullen.'

There is no record of the logical 'We want no Henry either' ever being

Foot combat armour of Henry VIII

voiced. He enjoyed an almost mystical personal popularity. He was to do many things far more reprehensible than putting away a wife who had given him only one daughter, in a marriage which it seemed even the Pope in Rome could not decide about, but he never lost his popularity with his people, and long after he had rotted in his grave, men seeing his daughter, Elizabeth, for the first time would shed tears because she so reminded them of her father.

It is significant that the one physical attack made on Anne, an assault that could have resulted in her death or in serious injury, took place when she went without Henry's protective presence to a supper-party in a Thameside house. A mob of women, reinforced by a few men dressed as women, raided the house, their intent, they said, to kill her. She was hustled into a boat and rowed to the other side of the river. She had escaped with her life, but the effect of such an experience on a highly strung, rather hysterical woman can be imagined. In her own eyes she had done nothing to warrant the people's hostility. She was not, as most married women regarded her, a stealer of another woman's husband; she had not sought the King's favour, he had sought hers. The feeling of being wronged would do nothing to sweeten her temper and in one of her tirades Henry was heard to remark that Katharine would never have spoken to him in that manner. An absurd complaint since he had chosen Anne for her difference from, not her resemblance to, Katharine.

Still, on the whole Henry bore, for a man of his temperament, the long waiting, his love's uncertain moods and the sexual frustration with astonishing patience. He sincerely longed for a legal annulment. He might allow his emissaries at Rome to drop a hint that unless the decision was made soon – and in his favour – he would be obliged to resort to other means. But such a threat was on a par with Clement's threat of excommunication; neither Pope nor King was anxious to apply the ultimate sanction. Clement did not want to see England invaded by either Francis or the Emperor; Henry did not want to defy Papal authority.

So the waiting went on, and to please Anne, to compensate her for the long delay, Henry decided to give her a singular honour, one never before granted to a woman.

Design for a triumphal arch for the coronation of Anne Boleyn

7

Queen at Last

She had the royal makings of a Queen.

HENRY VIII: *Shakespeare*

In England, as in other feudal countries, rank and title belonged to men able and ready to fight for the King and bring a muster of underlings to do the same: therefore no woman held rank *in her own right*. Henry had steadily advanced Anne's father, creating him finally Earl of Wiltshire and she was known as Lady Anne Rochford. Now she was to have a grander title, independent of her father or any other man. She was to be Marquis of Pembroke, with the right to take precedence over all other marquises, and she was to have manors and lands which guaranteed her an income of £1,000 a year.

The ceremony of ennoblement took place on 1 September 1532 at Windsor Castle, in the presence of the French Ambassador who had brought Francis's seemingly friendly advice, and of the Dukes of Norfolk and Suffolk and many peers of the realm.

Anne wore a gown of crimson velvet chosen to match the mantle of rank which the King would presently put over her shoulders, and she was attended by well-born ladies; Elizabeth, Countess of Rutland, Dorothy, Countess of Sussex and her own cousin, Norfolk's daughter, Lady Mary Howard. Her head was bare, ready for the coronet to be placed upon it, and the lustrous black hair streamed down past her waist.

Stephen Gardiner who had tried hard to get the annulment, and been made Bishop of Winchester as a reward, read out the patent of nobility which was remarkable in conferring a male title upon a female and for one notable omission. Such titles, the ordinary patent said, could be inherited by male heirs, *legally begotten*. In this case those words were omitted and as Henry placed the ermine-furred mantle round Anne's shoulders and the coronet upon her head, speculation ran rife. Was the King preparing, well in advance, for another bastard who would inherit his mother's title? Had Anne at last given in, and was this her reward? Or had Henry at last

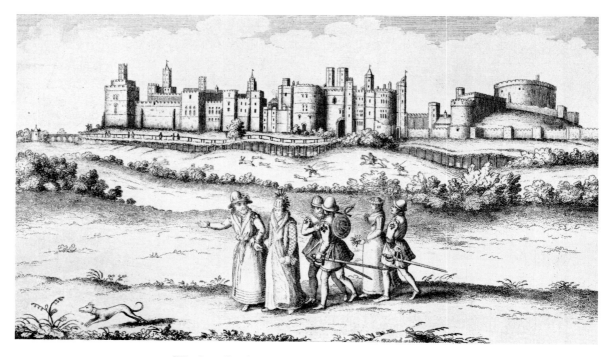

ABOVE Windsor Castle where Anne was created Marquis of Pembroke
OPPOSITE A sketch by Holbein of jewelry worn at the Tudor Court

despaired of ever being able to marry her, and chosen this very grand and
very public way of getting rid of her – paying off a discarded mistress?

Many people believed so firmly that she was Henry's mistress that a
story of a pregnancy, ended in a miscarriage, was going the rounds. Apart
from everything else this story must be denied by Henry's determination
to marry her. There had been enough miscarriages in his marital life; he
would never have married and been certain of an heir by a woman who
had once miscarried.

Anne knew that Henry was not preparing a title for a boy born out of
wedlock; she may have entertained a few fears about his preparing to
abandon her, but it is more likely that she recognized the ceremony for
what it was – partly a lover's gesture and partly a preparation for the
forthcoming visit to France, upon which she was to accompany him.

Francis and Henry were to meet again after nine years. The old rivalry
still existed and now they had something else to feel competitive about.
Queen Claude was dead and Francis had a new young Queen, Leore,
against whom Henry could show, not a young mistress, but a Queen-to-

be, graceful, well dressed, dignified, and wearing, symbolically, the jewels of the Queen of England.

Katharine had been forced to hand them over, though she, like Wolsey with the Great Seal, had refused to take a verbal order. Henry had been obliged to scrawl his signature to a command which left Katharine with only two ornaments, her wedding-ring and a thick gold chain which her mother had given her before she sailed from Corunna. Everybody knew who was to be the next wearer of the Queen's Jewels, and it may have been on this occasion that one of Katharine's attendants, forbidden to say a word against Henry, cursed Anne, and Katharine said, 'Curse her not, rather pity her.'

Not that there was anything pitiable about Anne as she made ready to go to France, a country she loved and of which she had happy memories despite the fact that there she had been obscure and poor. Nobody but a saint – which Anne never pretended to be – could have resisted the temptation to rejoice in going back to the same country, seeing some of the same people in circumstances so much altered for the better.

She must have felt very confident then. Henry's intention to take her with him proved that, as Chapuys acidly said, he could not do without her for an hour. His giving her Katharine's jewels was surely symbolic and he was going to talk with Francis who seemed in favour of the new marriage.

Then came the cruel snub.

If Anne went to France, she must be properly received. By whom? The Queen of France could not possibly be expected to meet a woman of dubious reputation. The King of France's sister, Marguerite, now Queen of Navarre, whom Anne was eager to meet again because it was in her household that her happy days had been spent, said privately that she did not wish to meet 'the King of England's whore' but publicly announced that she was too ill to undertake the duty. The Duchess of Vendôme? Her reputation was already so tarnished that she could meet Anne without suffering much damage. Henry was greatly affronted and decided that there would be no reception in France; Anne would go with him to Calais – still English soil – and he would go by himself to Boulogne where he would meet Francis.

Francis had again asked that display and splendour and retinues should be kept to the minimum and Henry had, as in 1514, decided otherwise, but now he reduced his following. It was impressive enough, however, and it included scholars and churchmen who had decided that he had never been legally married, and a Jew, brought from Venice because he had interpreted Leviticus to Henry's liking.

While Henry visited Francis I, Anne stayed at Calais which was still English soil

Henry went on to French soil and met Francis at Boulogne and was splendidly entertained. Anne stayed in Calais, her beautiful dresses and jewels all wasted. Henry missed her and the snub recently administered must have rankled within him, playing some small part in the decision he reached in a few days. Outwardly the talks went well, with Francis still advising Henry to ignore the Pope and marry.

Chapuys, the Spanish Ambassador, was not in France but he had a spy there – or perhaps he relied upon that unnamed 'certain gentleman'. The Emperor received a report that the Kings of France and England had agreed that if the Pope did not at once give the verdict in Henry's favour, or send the case back to England to be tried, they would *both* rebel against him. Whether Francis ever went quite so far, or if he did, meant what he said is questionable; certainly the French visit was a turning-point in Anne's life.

Did Henry say, in his infatuated way, when telling her that protocol demanded that she stay in Calais; 'Nevertheless, sweetheart, you shall meet the King of France'? It is possible. Having been entertained by Francis, Henry must entertain Francis on English soil, in Calais. Francis spent three days there. Being a man he could meet a woman of undefined status without being forever contaminated; at a masked ball he actually danced with her without suffering any damage. After the masks were removed, he talked to her for a long time.

Francis went back to Paris; Henry and Anne were prevented from sailing to England by the bad weather. There is strong evidence that during this time Anne did give in and admit Henry to her bed.

These few lines, listed as anonymous, are often attributed to Henry:

> Western wind when wilt thou blow,
> The small rain down can rain?
> Christ, if my love were in my arms
> And I in my bed again!

The lines may well have been Henry's, they chime with the raw longing expressed in some of his letters. And now, for Anne, the time of surrender was as ripe as it would ever be. By bringing her with him to France, by giving her the jewels of the Queen of England, by his hot resentment of the snub she had suffered, he had eventually proved his good faith. Whatever happened, he intended to marry her.

Conversely she may have surrendered from sheer desperation; time was running out, and she was – the one thing she had in common with Katharine – a gambler. She had played every card and was left with the last – yield to Henry and hope, *hope* that the union resulted in a son.

From her portrait she looks at us, large dark eyes, very knowing, a trifle world-weary, the mouth curved, more a sneer than a smile. The whole thing says: You will never know!

If yielding had been a gamble, it was a lucky one. By the middle of January 1533, Anne was sure enough of her condition to tell Henry that she was pregnant. He was delighted, but still in a difficult position. The coming child *must* be born in wedlock; therefore Henry must marry Anne. And officially he was still married to Katharine. Was he, after all this time about to be forced to commit what looked like bigamy?

He had the machinery for his release ready at hand. Warham the rather obstructionist old Archbishop of Canterbury had died in the August of the previous year and Henry had nominated Cranmer as his successor. Very properly the Pope had been informed, and the Papal Bull confirming Cranmer's appointment should have reached England by now. Once again, delay at Rome was being the obstacle. As soon as Cranmer was installed – with the Pope's blessing, he would be in a position of authority

ABOVE A travelling communion set of silver in a leather-covered box
OPPOSITE Clock presented to Anne Boleyn by Henry in 1532

and he had already indicated that he would use it as Henry wished. Cranmer did not regard Henry's first marriage as legal – and he was supported in this opinion by many of the universities. As Archbishop of Canterbury Cranmer would have power to convene an English court, but first he must be accepted by the Pope. Those who say that Henry broke with the Church of Rome lightly ignored the tremendous efforts he made to remain within the Church of Rome – and yet to have his own way.

They must be married, but secretly, furtively.

It was such a secret wedding that neither the place nor the name of the officiating priest is known. It took place very early on a January morning, either at Whitehall or at Greenwich, and the man who declared them to be man and wife till death did them part, may have been either Rowland Hill, one of the King's chaplains, or an Augustinian friar named George Browne – both men were given promotion soon afterwards. Anne's father, mother and brother were there, and there were two of her ladies. Her uncle, the Duke of Norfolk, always strenuously denied that he was present but said that some members of the King's Council were. He declined to name them. Cranmer was not there. It was as Chapuys called it a hole-and-corner affair, taking place in the drear early morning light of January, bereft of all splendour and of the right that even the humblest of women had – to look her best, to be fêted on her wedding day. But presently – and no doubt Henry promised this – the Coronation would be glorious enough to make up for this bleak, hastily performed affair.

Nothing was openly said, yet both Anne and Henry felt a compulsion to talk about it indirectly. When people came asking favours or wishing Anne to use her influence with the King, she told them that they must wait until she was married. She almost announced her pregnancy – a condition that could not be hidden indefinitely, by telling Thomas Wyatt and anyone else within hearing, that she had an overwhelming longing for apples, this in dead winter when apples were scarce – and that the King had said that such unseasonable longings were a sign of pregnancy. Then she laughed, so nobody could be sure whether she was serious or not.

Henry was equally indiscreet; he gave Anne a great quantity of silver plate, displayed in a cupboard – and to the Tudors a cupboard meant just what its name implies, not a space with a door but some open shelves. And at a dinner-party, glancing at the cups and dishes he asked was not this lady a good match, so richly endowed?

Clement behaved in exact accordance with the Biblical order not to let the right hand know what the other is doing. He sent a specially appointed messenger to deliver into Henry's hand an order to abandon Anne and take Katharine back, or be excommunicated by a given date. And at the same time he sent confirmation of Cranmer's office as Archbishop of Canterbury. Henry found little difficulty in avoiding the man who carried the threat, but he and Cranmer took instant advantage of the other Bull.

Before Cranmer was publicly consecrated in St Stephen's Church, he went into an adjoining room, and there before selected witnesses, swore that he did not intend to keep any oath of obedience to the Pope if it involved going against the law of the land, the will of the King, or the law of God. He then went into the church itself and there took all the traditional, conventional oaths. But he added something. As soon as he was indisputably Archbishop of Canterbury, he announced that everything he had just promised was subject to the protestation he had made just before the ceremony. So that everyone might understand, he read the protestation aloud, twice.

The law of the land could be changed by Act of Parliament; the law of God was – as Henry had argued, open to different interpretations; what remained was the will of the King, positive and unshakeable. He wanted, with all possible speed, to have his non-marriage ended and his marriage to Anne acknowledged. Towards this end everything, after the long stagnation, began to move swiftly. A complaisant Parliament passed an Act vesting the Archbishop of Canterbury with all spiritual power in England, Henry called his Council together and told those who did not know or had not guessed, that he and Anne were already married and that she would be crowned after Easter. Anne's brother George went to France to inform Francis and Francis replied with congratulations. An imposing deputation called upon Katharine – now moved from The More to a slightly less comfortable and accessible manor at Ampthill, not far from Dunstable – to tell her that Anne was now Henry's wife and about to

Petition of divorce from Henry VIII to Pope Clement VII concerning his marriage to Katharine of Aragon

be crowned Queen of England. Therefore Katharine must cease to use that title and accept instead that of Dowager Princess of Wales.

As she had done before, Katharine treated this order with contempt though the inducements to accept were considerable; if she would only accept she could see her daughter, she could choose her own residence, enjoy an enhanced income. Nothing moved her; she said she was Queen of England and would be deaf to anyone who addressed her by any other title, and, the time having come when her servants needed new clothes, she ordered that their jerkins should be embroidered, just as before, with Henry's initial and her own, linked.

If Anne actually hated Katharine as much as she is said to have done, it would be understandable; but there is no real evidence that she ever took any action against her. When Henry moved Katharine to less and less comfortable places, Buckden, and then Kimbolton, Anne had already lost her hold upon him. And why should she mind so much what Katharine chose to be called, and with what pattern she had her servants' coats embroidered, somewhere out in the wilds?

In London the apartments in the Tower, the place from which, by tradition, all Kings and Queens went to be crowned, were being prepared for the Coronation; fresh plaster, painting, gilding, glazing, new carpets and hangings, even a new door giving upon a private garden. Everything that Anne had planned when Henry made his first overtures, had come about. She was pregnant – both she and Henry were certain that the child would be a son, heir to England; Cranmer was about to open his court at Dunstable, which Katharine could attend if she wished, the distance being not great, or ignore if she felt so disposed, as she had ignored the much more imposing court at Blackfriars. The verdict was certain. By the standards of the time it was a brief session; it opened on 10 May and on 13 May gave its verdict: Henry had never been legally married to Katharine; he had, therefore, been a bachelor when he married Anne. So she was Queen of England, her child would be legitimate. This was what she had insisted upon and what Henry had worked and connived for.

In the triumph, the long wooing rewarded, the fairy-tale come true, the near-impossible attained, there were only two discordant notes.

One was struck publicly. In many churches when the moment came to pray for the King and the Queen, with Anne's name in place of Katharine's, a great many people simply walked out. Henry could deal with that; he sent for the Lord Mayor of London and scolded him; he was to see that such a thing never happened again; he was to send for all the Heads of the various Guilds and give them orders which they were to pass on to their employees and apprentices, and *their wives*. Anything, word or act, derogatory to Queen Anne was to be a punishable offence. And the streets of the city were to be prepared for the Coronation. Cleaned, freshly gravelled, in places roped off so that spectators could stand in safety. And there were to be at salient places what were called 'pageants' which we think of as moving shows, but in the sixteenth century meant something more static, an erection of a decorative or symbolic nature, an elevation from which speeches could be made, or songs sung. Even groups of people who were not citizens of London – such as the merchants of the Hanseatic League – were to spend money on making a suitable display.

That was Henry's public reaction to anything that seemed like a slight to his beloved. Why then, did he in private make such a fuss about what barge she chose to use for her triumphal progress by river to the Tower on the eve of her Coronation?

The barge was Katharine's own and still bore the arms of Spain when Anne made the perfectly natural decision to take it, have it stripped of the Royal insignia and decorated with her own which had been rather hastily concocted for her when she became Marquis of Pembroke. She had taken Katharine's husband, and her jewels, was about to take her Crown: why not her barge? Henry was angry when he heard about it and spoke roughly to Anne's Chamberlain, saying the barge was Katharine's and there were plenty of other barges available.

This piece of gossip, duly reported to the Emperor by Chapuys was not derived from that vague 'certain gentleman' but from the Duke of Norfolk: it has the ring of truth, too trivial to have been invented. It is one of the things which leads to the suspicion that the marriage, so long awaited, so eagerly worked for, had not proved as satisfactory as Henry had hoped. Henry's anger could hardly have been due to sentiment about Katharine whom he was keeping in virtual imprisonment, from whom he demanded the Queen's Jewels, whose status as Queen and married woman he gone to such lengths to deny. It was anger with Anne; the kind of petty fault-finding that stems from a deeper grudge.

He could hardly scold Anne and provoke a hysterical scene; she was five months pregnant with what he was certain would be the longed-for heir, so he spoke roughly to the Chamberlain who had merely obeyed her orders. In the early autumn of 1532, he had been only too pleased to load her with Katharine's jewels from which Katharine might still derive some pleasure; now in May 1533 he was quibbling about the use of a barge for which Katharine, immured at Ampthill, had no use at all. And all that had

Decorated barge supposed to have belonged to Henry VIII

happened which could explain his change of attitude, was that in the interval she had admitted him to her bed.

Perhaps he had expected too much; something wonderful, out of this world. Perhaps she was not a very satisfactory bed-partner. Her behaviour during those years of waiting hints strongly that she was undersexed. There must have been summer evenings in scented gardens when an ordinary woman, however hard-headed, would have found it difficult to allow an urgent lover every favour except the last. And Henry himself, after so long a self-enforced celibacy, may not immediately have become quite the purveyor of joy whom Katharine, Bessie Blount and Mary Boleyn remembered.

One is almost forced to believe – not least from his eventual viciousness towards her – that Henry, having attained the seemingly unattainable, and paid a heavy price for it, was disappointed. And that Anne, her aim achieved, against almost overwhelming odds, became more self-confident. She was about to be crowned; in September, she would be brought to bed with a son.

The coronation procession of Anne Boleyn past Westminster Cathedral. Although the streets were crowded, few cheers were heard for Anne

She had, in all but one respect, a splendid Coronation, beginning on Thursday, 29 May, when she was rowed, in the disputed barge, from Greenwich to the Tower. Forty other barges, all wonderfully decorated and belonging to important people, formed an escort, and hundreds of humbler craft, some dangerously overcrowded, were there. People came to stare, but not to cheer. The silence of the mob was obscured by the music – every escorting barge had its musicians; there was gun-firing, too,

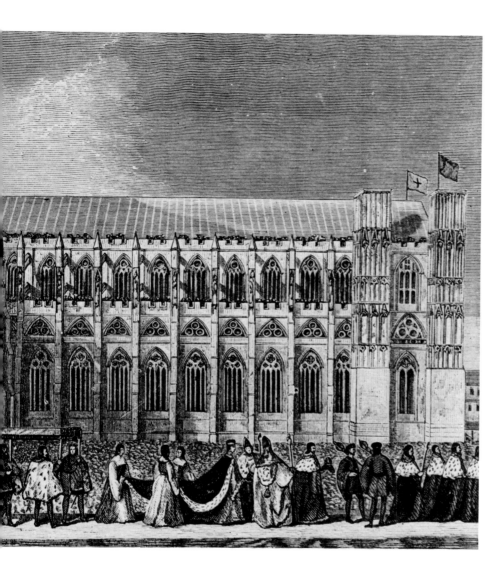

and one barge which Anne especially noted, was hung all over with little bells which tinkled.

It was a fine, bright day, and she wore a dress of glittering cloth of gold. The shining black waterfall of hair fell to below her waist: she 'sat in her hair', Cranmer said; against its darkness, jewels sparkled. Above her barge her own personal emblem floated – a white falcon rising from a bough of Tudor roses. All the other barges displayed the banners of their owners,

Music is played as guests wait for the feasting to begin

lengths of gay bunting, bright ribbons, wreaths of flowers.

Other unpopular monarchs have enjoyed a fleeting popularity by being the centre of some great spectacle, especially if the occasion also promises feasts and free wine; but even this lessening of animosity was not granted to Anne. The ceremony that was to make her Queen of England had begun, but to the people on the small river-boats and round the landing-stage at the Tower, she was still Nan Bullen and they wanted none of her.

The cannon from the Tower boomed a welcome; she landed with her ladies and was received by the Constable of the Tower and his Lieutenant

Stylized dance was part of the tradition of courtly love introduced into England by
Eleanor of Aquitaine and a strong influence at the court of Henry VIII

who led her to the King who smiled and embraced her in a manner several
observers noted, laying his hands on either side of her body. Even if
unconscious the gesture was significant – he was embracing the child!
King and Queen then retired, with a few privileged guests to the newly
decorated and furnished apartments and enjoyed a sumptuous supper.

To us all Tudor feasts sound gargantuan, consisting as they did of many
courses, fish, meat, game, puddings, sweetmeats, desserts; to qualify for
the adjective sumptuous this celebratory meal must have been a very
splendid feast indeed and probably included the first strawberries of the

season, gathered from the fields which then covered what is now the West End of London.

Anne made her river journey on Thursday, 29 May. Friday was spent partly in resting, and partly in entertaining at dinner the eighteen men who on Saturday were to be made Knights of the Bath. One of these was young Francis Weston, one day to be, with Anne, in the Tower in less happy circumstances. Over sixty other men were to be knighted in the ordinary way. Henry had spared nothing which might contribute to making the Coronation glorious.

On Saturday came the second traditional Coronation journey, this time by road, through the streets of the city, from the Tower to Westminster. Anne wore a gown and mantle of white tissue, furred with ermine, and a coronet of precious stones. She rode in a litter lined with cloth of silver, and the two animals which bore it were so draped about with the same material that nobody could be certain whether they were horses or mules. Four knights of the Cinque Ports, wearing the scarlet robes of their office carried a canopy of cloth of silver over the litter; the new Knights of the Bath wore blue. Equally splendid and colourful were the representatives of the City Guilds. There were ladies on horseback, wearing cloth of gold, and another magnificent litter was provided for ladies too old to ride. Chief among these was the Dowager Duchess of Norfolk, taking the place of her daughter-in-law. The Duchess, though Anne's aunt-by-marriage, was so passionately pro-Katharine that she refused to have anything to do with the Coronation of the usurper.

Every house was – by order – decorated with flags, tapestries, garlands. But, as Henry said later that day, he could order many things, but he could not make people cheer. There were few cheers, and so many men kept their hats on that Anne's Fool at one point cried, 'I think you all have scurvy heads and dare not uncover.'

Two of the pageants presented struck a discordant note. The Hanseatic merchants had chosen a representation of Apollo on Mount Parnassus, and the mound was decorated with coats of arms. Highest of all was the great black Eagle of the Emperor, with the arms of Spain on its breast – Katharine's emblem which had just been scraped from the barge; lower down was Henry's and lowest of all, Anne's. It was a subtle, but deliberate insult. One can imagine her thin, arched eyebrows coming together in a scowl as she realized the implication. Henry, too, was annoyed when he heard of it and swore he would punish the people responsible; but there was little he could do. The Hanseatic League was extremely powerful; it handled almost all the Baltic trade; its London headquarters, the

Merchant's mark showing the Tudor rose

Steelyard, was almost a fortress; and all its ships were fully armed.

The other discordant note was a mere blunder. The pageant at Leadenhall honoured St Anne, mother of the Virgin Mary. It was intended as a compliment to Anne, and an innocent, well-coached child made a little speech. St Anne had been 'a fruitful tree', and everybody hoped that her namesake would be likewise. The sting lay in the fact that St Anne was only remembered as being the mother of a daughter – and neither Henry nor Anne wished for a female child. Henry was quite certain that, the Levitical curse lifted, he would be given a son. And he had the assurances of all the soothsayers and fortune-tellers whom he had consulted. They said what they felt was required of them; the child would be a boy, a Prince of Wales at last. Not – and Henry must have remembered this at times – that seers were to be trusted. For Elizabeth Barton, the Holy Nun of Kent had issued a warning; if the King married Anne Boleyn, he would die. And here he was, married to her and still alive!

(But people in direct communication with God often speak in parables and in a certain sense the Holy Nun may have been right. There are other deaths than those of the body and from first to last, from the moment in 1523 when Henry first looked upon Anne and saw her as desirable, to the

Holbein drawing of a Court lady of the time

moment when he looked on her and saw her as wholly detestable, something in him had been dying as inexorably as his bodily tissue. A kind of spiritual death.)

Apart from the little jarring notes, everything about the Coronation went well. Anne ended her journey at Westminster and was there allowed to rest and was offered refreshments, which she passed on to her attendants. She may have been too much excited, or too exhausted to eat. On the whole, for a woman five months pregnant, and growing bulky under the fine raiment, she was bearing up wonderfully. She was having the easy pregnancy which old country midwives would interpret as an ominous sign. As late as 1942 old women, speaking with the voice of experience, of tradition, would tell an expectant mother suffering worse than ordinary pregnancy ills that she could count on a boy, since boys were more trouble, right from the start.

From Westminster Hall, Anne, taking a side entrance to avoid the gaping, but hostile crowds, went to Whitehall where Henry was again awaiting her. And on the next morning, Sunday 1 June in the year 1533, she went into Westminster Abbey to be crowned. This time she wore the purple velvet of royalty. Cranmer, Archbishop of Canterbury, anointed her on the palms of her hands, on her breast. St Edward's crown – very heavy on a head supported by such a slim neck – was put in place. Nothing of royalty was missing – the orb and the sceptre, one in this hand, one in the other. Plain Anne Boleyn, that foolish girl, deemed unfit to be a wife to an Earl's heir, was now Queen of England.

In this ceremony Henry took no part, but watched from a screened gallery. He could at least reflect that though Anne no longer enthralled him and was, therefore, capable of annoying him, her conduct and demeanour could not be faulted. No Princess reared and schooled for Queenship could have shown more grace and dignity.

8

The Act of Supremacy

If a lion knew his strength it were hard for any Man to rule him.

Sir Thomas More

That summer Anne did not accompany Henry on his Progress, and he contented himself by making short hunting trips, never away for long, never going far from Greenwich where Anne was awaiting the birth. He did his best to protect her from anything likely to disturb her peace of mind, yet things calculated to upset her had a way of drifting through.

She heard, for instance, of the scenes which took place when Katharine was moved from Ampthill to Buckden. The enthusiasm of the crowd had not waned. All along the route women stood weeping and men shouted, 'God save the Queen', asked how they could serve her and pronounced themselves willing to die for her. Mary moved from one manor to another at about the same time and was everywhere met by the same demonstrations of loyalty and affection.

About this, Henry could take action. He published an edict; it was henceforth a capital offence to address or refer to Katharine as Queen.

Then the Hanseatic merchants added to their insult by bringing into the Thames an unusually large number of ships which fired a defiant salvo under the very walls of Greenwich Palace and inviting Chapuys to a magnificent banquet on board one of the vessels. This just after the Emperor himself had written to his Ambassador, telling him to be more tactful in his dealings with Henry and not to do or say anything to jeopardize the friendship between the Emperor and England. Charles was, in fact, prepared to be conciliatory so long as the Eastern borders of his Empire were threatened by the Turks; he wanted to avoid a war on two fronts. But while refusing to support the Pope in anything he might say and do by armed might, Charles did give advice. The Pope should

OPPOSITE Cardinal John Fisher who went to the execution block rather than accept the Act of Supremacy

The Thames at Richmond. While Anne awaited the birth of her child, Henry only made short hunting trips in the summer of 1533

settle, with no further delay, this long-drawn-out question of who *was* Queen of England.

This Clement did in July, acting with the precipitance so often shown by the normally hesitant. He declared Henry's marriage to Anne null and void and said that if Henry had not left Anne and taken Katharine back by the end of September, he would be excommunicated. Not being a simpleton, Clement must have known that Henry would not put away a woman due to be delivered of his child sometime in September and take back his ageing wife. And he must have known that without some backing from a monarch willing to take advantage of an excommunicated monarch's plight, the threat had no teeth. It was a mere gesture.

Henry did his best to keep this bit of news from Anne and when he called his Privy Council and other advisers to meet him to discuss it, he chose Guildford as the place of meeting and told Anne that he was going to hunt at Windsor. But, of course, she was told; just as she was told something else. Henry had taken a mistress.

Of all the small mysteries which cling about the story, this is perhaps the most puzzling. The woman was never named, even by Chapuys, such a gossip, so well supplied with information. She was 'a lady about the Court', she was 'very beautiful'. No more.

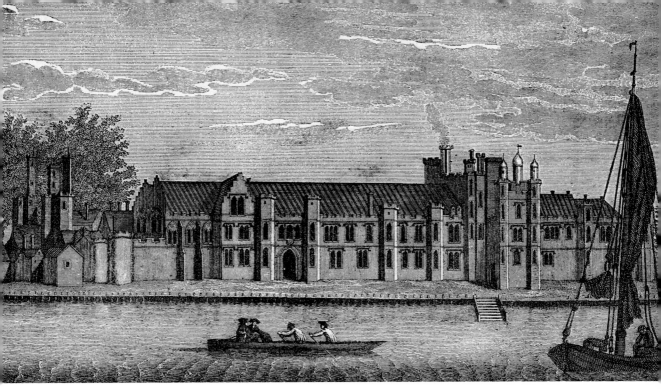

The old palace at Greenwich. It was here that the Hanseatic merchants registered their disapproval of Henry's marriage to Anne by firing their guns defiantly

The fact that Henry had taken a mistress should not have perturbed Anne unduly. Many men took mistresses when their wives were in the final, unattractive stages of pregnancy. Most women accepted the situation without complaint. Anne did not; she flew into a temper and Henry, momentarily forgetting his role, snapped back at her and told her to shut her eyes and endure as her betters – meaning Katharine – had done. But Anne was not Katharine; she had grown bulky, heavier and slower of movement; but her mind, her gift for finding the cutting phrase, had not been blurred by her physical condition. For two or three days she refused to speak to Henry. With the future Prince of Wales alive and kicking within her, she was in command again.

Years later, Elizabeth, daughter of this doomed marriage, was to say furiously to her Council, 'Had I been born crested, not cloven, you would not have dared speak to me thus!' She was born cloven – female – on the afternoon of Sunday, 7 September 1533, and except for Anne's enemies, everyone was disappointed. Even those who disapproved of the marriage might have become reconciled to it had it produced the longed-for heir.

Everything had been prepared for a boy, though the scribes who had the announcement ready had cautiously left a little space after prince so that two vital letters could be added. Even his name had been chosen: he

Quarry with the badge of Anne Boleyn – a white falcon rising from a bed of Tudor roses – in a stained-glass window in Wethersfield Church, Essex

was to be Edward after his great-grandfather, or Henry after his grandfather and father. The vast canopied cradle of estate, decorated with the Royal Arms and furnished with coverings all scarlet and blue and ermine, awaited him.

Most disappointed of all were the parents, but once again Henry's better side showed as it had when Mary was born. 'She will have brothers,' he said. And the indications were hopeful; this child had gone full time, appeared to be healthy and vigorous; Anne had had a good pregnancy and a normal labour. Within a year, with any luck …

Defying anybody to commiserate with him, Henry carried his daughter around and showed her off and arranged for her to have a splendid christening at which once again, the Dowager Duchess of Norfolk was chief lady, entrusted with the task of holding the baby whose purple robe had so long a train that it took four lords to carry it.

The noise of the heralds' voices and of the trumpets had scarcely died away before Henry was looking to the future and taking steps to make sure that Elizabeth's status should never be questioned by anybody, and never challenged by Mary.

That Katharine still regarded herself as Queen of England and repudiated the title of Dowager Princess of Wales no longer mattered much; she was forty-eight years old, in poor health and safely out of sight. Mary was different; only seventeen, surely she could be persuaded into admitting that she had no claim to the title of Princess.

So far, except that she was kept from Court and not allowed to see her mother, no great pressure had been brought to bear upon Mary. Now it was. Before Elizabeth was a month old, Mary was told that she must move from Beaulieu where she had lived in some splendour, to a relatively humble place; she was to be known as the Lady Mary and renounce the title of Princess. She would no longer have her own servants, wearing her own livery.

At first Mary pretended that she was sure that her father could never have ordered such a thing. She wrote to him; she was his lawful daughter, born in legal marriage. It was, in fact, Katharine all over again. And to Anne, who had so long insisted that her child should be legitimate and royal, Mary's attitude and some of the things she said were extremely exasperating and insulting. Mary was willing, she said, to accept Elizabeth as her half-sister, just as she had accepted the young Duke of Richmond as her half-brother. The meaning of that was clear – both were bastards. Just as offensive was Mary's habit of referring to Anne as Madame Pembroke.

In later years Anne was inclined to accuse herself of having treated Mary badly and it is an accusation frequently brought against her; in fact there seems little real substance for the charge. Even placid people when angered say things they do not mean – and Anne was far from placid. She said that she would humiliate Mary by bringing her back to Court, and making her carry her train; but that threat was never brought into effect and such a move – indeed any move – against Mary could not be made without Henry's consent. Of that, of the slavish desire to please, Anne could no longer be certain.

King and Queen slept together because they both hoped for an heir; and neither of them, being proud people, would admit that the marriage had failed, but Anne knew that she had lost her power. She probably knew exactly when and why, and suspected that Henry would not have pressed ahead with the marriage except for the fact that she was pregnant.

The one suggestion regarding Mary's future which Anne made at this time was certain of Henry's approval, for he was annoyed with his elder daughter, too, and wished to subdue her obstinate spirit. As a Princess, possible heir to the throne, Elizabeth was to have her own establishment, ruled over by Lady Shelton, who was Anne's aunt; and Mary was to join the household as a lady-in-waiting to her half-sister. That should make clear their relative positions. But Mary's certainty of her own rights had been strengthened in December when the Pope gave the verdict after ten years of indecision. He said that Julius's Dispensation was good and the marriage between Henry and Katharine sound and legal. Lady Shelton was to find the Lady Mary far from meek.

Elizabeth's household, like all others of any size, made frequent moves so that dwellings could be thoroughly cleaned and aired, but it was often at Hatfield in Hertfordshire, in the Old Palace of which only one wing now remains. The baby Princess in a splendid litter, splendidly escorted, went to her new home in December when she was three months old. In a shabby old litter, escorted by the Duke of Norfolk and so small a retinue as to attract no attention, Mary went the same way.

In the January of 1534 – a year which was to see many changes – Henry went to Hatfield to visit his infant daughter. He did not see Mary officially – Thomas Cromwell had visited her and reported that she was still intransigent – but as Henry was mounting to come away, Mary moved to a window or a balcony, in order to see him go. Early impressions are long-lasting and Mary probably cherished memories of a fond, indulgent, jovial father whose changed attitude towards herself and her mother could be directly attributed to the terrible influence of Anne Boleyn. Presently Henry was to treat Mary worse, and Elizabeth just as badly, yet they both prided themselves on being his daughters. Of all Henry's children the only one who gave least display of filial sentiment was the close-lipped, cold-hearted little boy whom he did at last beget.

Seeing Mary watching him, Henry raised his hat and bowed, and all

OPPOSITE Anne Boleyn's bedhead at Hever Castle

those with him did the same. This small gesture of half-recognition was promptly reported to Anne and she instructed her aunt that if Mary insisted upon her title of Princess, she should be slapped on the face, 'like the cursed bastard she was'.

To us it sounds extreme, but physical chastisement was a commonplace in Tudor times; parents beat their children, masters beat servants, masters beat schoolboys. The Duke of Norfolk said that had he had a daughter as stubborn as Mary he would have banged her head against the wall until it was as soft as a baked apple. There is no record of Lady Shelton carrying out this order. She must have been a rather exceptional woman. She owed her comfortable post to Anne, yet she was bold enough to say that Mary had virtues that should be honoured. Both Katharine and Mary had the knack which Anne lacked – that of attracting women friends.

In March 1534 Anne, despite the fact that she was again pregnant, went to Hatfield herself, holding out the olive branch to Mary. She was prepared to say that if Mary would be obliging, she should come back to Court, not to carry Anne's train, but to take precedence – she should walk by the Queen's side, even through doorways. This unprecedented concession was wasted. Mary shut herself in her room, refused to meet Madame Pembroke, saying she could recognize no Queen but her own mother.

It is possible, even likely, that the journey, and the rage which failure invoked, brought about Anne's first miscarriage.

The repeated pattern of miscarriages – Katharine had at least six and Anne had three – the incurable sore on Henry's leg, the poor health of his surviving children has led to the suggestion that he suffered from syphilis. It was then a mysterious disease, even its place of origin uncertain. Some held that the Portuguese brought it from Africa, others that Columbus and his followers from the New World. No European country would own it; the English called it the French or the Italian pox; in Europe it was known as the English pox. Both the symptoms and the mortality rate were more severe in Tudor times than they are even with untreated cases today.

If Henry suffered from it and Katharine's miscarriages were the result of it, he must have contracted it early in life. But when, and how? Until his father's death he led the life of an over-supervised schoolboy and as soon as he decently could married Katharine for whom he had a romantic love. He most probably came to her virgin, as she claimed that she came to him.

Well into middle age he enjoyed exceptionally good health and vigour, was renowned for his skill in the tilt-yard and on the tennis-court; and in a

Henry was always enthusiastic about real tennis and was skilled at the game

day's hunting he could tire out five or six strong horses. There is no mention of his suffering from any mysterious illness or of his being obliged to refrain from public appearances – except when he suffered from smallpox and, treated in the ordinary way, recovered well. He had in his time several false friends, and some virulent enemies. One feels that had he been syphilitic the word would have been used against him by somebody, at some time. The sore on his leg may well have resulted from a hurt he received in a tournament, memorable for another reason, when he was forty-five years old and slightly too old to be riding in tourneys at all, and when flesh heals more slowly. And he certainly never suffered from the tertiary stage of syphilis, paralysis and insanity.

We look at his children and their poor health.

Mary, born in 1516, was normal, precocious, lively and intelligent. She died at the age of forty-two of a stomach tumour which – almost to the end – she was sure was a pregnancy.

Bessie Blount's son, the Duke of Richmond, born in 1519, showed no sign of the saddle nose or the jagged teeth of a child fathered by a syphilitic. He died when he was seventeen, wasted by what sounds like tuberculosis.

Edward VI lived only sixteen years and died of the same disease.

Elizabeth's health was extremely variable: on good days she could hunt all day and dance far into the night; on bad ones she suffered from incapacitating headaches and severe palpitations of the heart, symptoms more psychosomatic than syphilitic; and she died in her seventieth year.

There must be some significance in the fact that Henry's mistress – to whom her child's sex was not important, carried her child full-time. Both Katharine and Anne bore living daughters full-time, and then, under stress – at the time an unrecognized enemy – began to miscarry.

Alongside the question of whether or not Henry was syphilitic, arises another; was he, or did he become, impotent? At her trial, among accusations of crimes so infamous that only a woman out of her mind could have committed them, was the accusation that she and her brother had joked about Henry's impotence.

It is only of importance here because it *may*, just possibly, have influenced her behaviour. Pure surmise, of course, but worth a moment's consideration.

Henry no longer loved her; he came to her bed now as a duty rather than as a pleasure, and two of the babies thus begotten had come to nothing. Her first miscarriage came in January 1534, her second in June. Did she, in desperation, take another man, a more promising sire to her bed?

If she did, poor Mark Smeaton could have been a likely choice. A man of humble origin, admitted to Court circles because he was such a good musician, extremely good-looking, and a person whose comings and goings were less closely scrutinized than those of more important men.

From a medical text of the early sixteenth century showing some of the ingredients used in preparing medicines

Præparatoria   Maheleb.   Aqua Cam-   Vsuem.   Ciperi.   Sandalus albus,   Rosæ.
Dentium.   phoræ.   & rubeus.

And it was a belief at the time that the country-bred were the best begetters of sons. Seven boys might contend for a blacksmith's forge or a saw-mill, or a few acres and a donkey. The truth lay shrouded – poor women breast-fed their babies and that tilted the survival scales in favour of the boys who in gestation and the first months of life were the more delicate. The handsome young son of a carpenter may have seemed to her a promising sire of the son which she so desperately needed if she wanted to retain the Crown. She knew Henry well by this time and she had seen how he had dealt with a wife who had given him no son – and whom he had ceased to love.

The *canard* about Anne having taken Smeaton as a lover lasted longer than the others. Mary sometimes said that Elizabeth resembled him in looks. Mary can have had no head for figures; Mark Smeaton did not meet Anne until three months before Elizabeth's birth. And when the adult Elizabeth began to appear in public men turned aside and wept because she so much reminded them of her father, the King they had revered while he lived, and whose memory they still cherished.

That Mark Smeaton confessed to adultery with the Queen, must be discounted; he made the confession under torture, when men will say anything. Anne denied it to the end, even with death and the Day of Judgment waiting her.

That Henry had ceased to have any feeling for Anne, except as a brood mare, was made plain in various ways. He renewed his attentions to that lady who was never named. The only thing we know about her is that she was not Jane Seymour, Jane was not a lady of the Court at the time.

The Boleyn family who had done so well out of their connection with Anne, titles and honours, manors, and remunerative posts, were aware of the changed climate and thought that if the King must take a mistress, it might as well be a woman of their clan. So Margaret Shelton, the daughter of Lady Shelton, head of Elizabeth's household, was brought to Court. She was young, fair and amenable and moderately successful. But Henry had more on his mind at the moment than mere light flirtation.

In Anne herself he may have lost interest, no longer finding any charm in the very qualities which had once entranced him, but he was determined that her right to be Queen, and that the legitimacy of Elizabeth – and any other child she might bear, should be acknowledged by everyone. Parliament was forced into passing the Act of Succession and all Henry's subjects were compelled to take an oath that they accepted it. The close and intricate networks of clerical and secular authority went to work; the

Archbishop of Canterbury administered the oath to Bishops and they to lesser clergy; Heads of Guilds and Crafts swore on behalf of their members; Mayors of towns, Sheriffs of counties did the same. With death the penalty for refusing or protesting, opposition was minimal. To say in a disgruntled moment – as one man did – that the weather had not been good since the good old Queen was put away, was to be persecuted and condemned.

The Act of Succession predated the Act of Supremacy, and made it inevitable. Even Henry must have seen that. It was impossible to force the people of England to accept Anne as Queen, her children as legitimate when the Pope had decreed otherwise, without denying Papal authority altogether. This Henry did by means of an Act which made him Head of the Church and forbade the sending of any revenues to Rome.

There were people who were relieved by the freedom from payment of Peter's Pence – the levy of a penny a year on every hearth, except one, in every house. Relief from these taxes was short-lived; it was soon learned that the King meant to replace them with taxes of his own. It was to this that Anne made tart reference during one of her quarrels with Henry; she told him that he should be grateful to her for enriching him.

Henry was astute enough to see that the Act of Supremacy could open the door to a flood of Lutheranism – or Protestantism as it was beginning to be called. And despite everything he still regarded himself as a good Catholic whom the Pope had treated badly, forcing him into schism. At heart he was still the man who had gained the title of Defender of the Faith by writing a book called *A Defence of the Seven Sacraments*, a direct answer to Luther's attack on Holy Church. To the end of his reign Henry was as ready to persecute Protestant heretics as he was to persecute those who would not accept the Act of Supremacy. When Clement died in September 1534, Henry immediately opened negotiations with his successor, Paul III, offering to bring England back into the Church of Rome if only the Pope would reverse Clement's decision about the marriage. This, Paul – a far rockier character than Clement – refused to do, and early in 1535, he did something calculated to infuriate Henry. He made John Fisher, Bishop of Rochester, a Cardinal.

Fisher, Thomas More, and several other people were in the Tower because they had refused to accept the Act of Supremacy.

About the Act of Succession people might cherish strong feelings, either because they were pro-Katharine, or foresighted enough to see that

OPPOSITE Elizabeth, the daughter of Henry VIII and Anne Boleyn, as a princess

ANNO DÑI · 1·5·4·4·

LADI MARI DOVGHTER TO
THE MOST VERTVOVS PRINCE
KING HENRI THE EIGHT

THE AGE OF XXVIII YERES

ABOVE Holbein's drawing of a merchant, the sort of person who would have resented greatly the payment of Peter's Pence
OPPOSITE Mary I, the daughter of Henry VIII and Katharine of Aragon

the substitution of Elizabeth for Mary as heir could involve a long minority – almost always disastrous for a country. But it was not a matter about which most people felt strongly enough to invite martyrdom.

The Act of Supremacy was different. It touched upon matters of principle, or belief, the kind of thing for which some men were willing to die. John Fisher, always a supporter of Katharine, and Thomas More, neutral in that particular matter, had both refused to accept the Act of Supremacy, and when the new Pope made Fisher a Cardinal, Henry swore that he would send the head to Rome to fit the hat – that great wide tasselled hat of the exact pattern which Wolsey had worn on State occasions.

Yet Henry did not act at once; he did not immediately order Fisher to be tried and executed as a traitor and have his head sent to Rome. He showed, in fact, the extraordinary patience which his daughter, Elizabeth, was later to show towards Mary Queen of Scots and which he had shown in his long wooing of Anne Boleyn.

Fisher and More had been sent to the Tower, and at first leniently treated; they could have books and writing materials; friends and relatives could visit them; and they were allowed to walk in one of the several enclosed gardens. Later, gentle means and persuasion having failed, conditions had been made more rigorous; nothing to read, nothing with which to write, no visitors, no strolls in the garden. But no amount of deprivation or hardship could change their minds. The Pope, whatever his personal behaviour – and some Popes had been very bad – was Head of the Church, endowed with authority and power and something more – the mystical link that ran back, through St Peter, to Christ himself.

Fisher and More took their stand, and so did many heads of religious establishments, monasteries, priories, convents, friaries.

Henry attacked one of the most powerful of the various Orders – the Carthusians. Those who were to be punished as an example of what would happen to those who would not accept Henry as Head of the Church were carefully chosen, so that the terror might be widespread. There was a Prior from London, one from Lincolnshire, one from Nottinghamshire. These, with a few others including a humble parish priest, went to the Tower and were vilely treated – chained to stone pillars in such a position that they could neither stand upright, sit, nor lie down. They were also kept short of food. At the end of this ordeal – steadfast to the end – they were dragged on hurdles to Tyburn, where the Marble Arch now stands, and there they suffered the long-drawn-out death reserved for traitors. They were hanged until they were almost dead but cut down while still conscious and then eviscerated – their vital organs torn out and burned before their eyes.

As an exercise in terrorism it failed, for while the men were dealt with one by one, so that those awaiting execution could see what it meant, nobody recanted. One spectator noted that they did not even change colour or become silent from horror. To the last man the exhortation went on. The King must be obeyed in all things except those which were contrary to the honour of God, and of Holy Church.

The Tower of London by Anthony van der Wyngaerde. Cardinal Fisher, Sir Thomas More, and later Anne herself, were kept prisoner here before their execution. The heads of Fisher and More were displayed on spikes on Tower Bridge

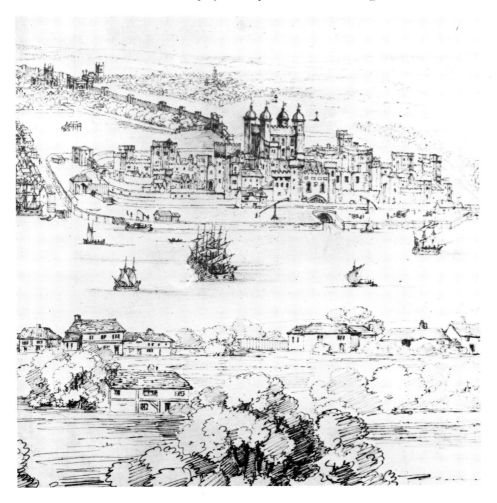

Tho: Moor Ld Chancelour

ABOVE Massacre of the Carthusians by Henry VIII showing the tortures to which they were subjected

OPPOSITE Although a close friend of Henry, Sir Thomas More refused to sacrifice his conscience to the Act of Supremacy, forcing Henry to sentence him to death

That was in May 1535. Fisher was allowed another month, and Thomas More two. Neither recanted and the law must take its course. About Fisher Henry probably had little personal feeling; Fisher had always been against the annulment of the marriage with Katharine, and against the marriage with Anne. Still, Henry had no wish to make a martyr of him because he was venerated, even in Protestant countries, for his learning and his saintliness.

Thomas More was rather different. He had been as near an intimate friend as a King could have. Henry had always enjoyed hard physical exercise and the competitiveness of the joust and the tennis-court; but he

Dicing and playing cards, 1525

had his scholarly side too, and he had delighted in More's company, the witty, urbane conversation, the learning, the sheer charm. Also, not to be ignored, was the fact that More belonged to the past. At the age of forty-three, his personal life unsatisfactory and his public affairs bristling with problems, Henry was in a state of mind to look back and see a glamorized past; see himself walking with More in the riverside garden and talking about everything under the sun, and in the heavens above. *Before all this trouble began.*

However, to refuse to acknowledge the Act of Supremacy was treason, so Fisher and More must die. They were to be spared the atrocities that attended the execution of the Carthusians, and were to be beheaded. Fisher went to his death in June 1535, More in July. Perhaps even at that late hour Henry hoped that More would swear and save his life.

Fisher had always been a lean man, but he was now skeletally thin and when his head was exposed on a spike on Tower Bridge, it did not corrupt or attract the carrion-eating birds. In a state of mummification, it stayed there until people began to regard its condition as a manifestation of the supernatural; then somebody took it down and dropped it into the Thames.

Fisher had made a moving speech from the scaffold, so when More's turn came he was told to be brief. Brief he was. Confronting the headsman with the axe and the crowd come to watch, More said, 'I die the King's good servant – but God's first.'

The news was brought to Henry when he was playing some dicing game; Anne stood near, watching. He turned to her and said with venom, 'It is because of you the honestest man in my kingdom is dead!' He threw down the dice and would play no more.

Those few words show with painful clarity, the state of feeling between them. He knew now the cost of getting his own way, and blamed her. Yet the marriage must continue, on the chance of producing a living, male baby. King and Queen must bed together. Even if Anne had, in desperation, resorted to some other man, even if Henry, now hating what he had loved, were partially impotent, he must be deluded into thinking that any child she bore was fathered by him. She must have managed this tricky business very cleverly indeed for when she miscarried for the last, fatal time, Henry said, 'You will get no more sons by me', an acknowledgment that what he had fathered, the little lost thing, far enough gestated to make his sex certain, had been, in Henry's eyes, his son.

9

Accusations, Arrest and Imprisonment

Alas it pitieth me – to think into what misery she will shortly come.

Sir Thomas More

That summer's Progress – Anne's last – took the Court far afield, to the border of Wales, a country for which Henry cherished a sentimental affection because a Welsh prince figured in his ancestry and Tudor was actually a Welsh name. Away from his capital – where policy ruled, and blood had been shed, his spirit revived and his temper sweetened. He enjoyed the hunting and the various entertainments provided for him. Anne, though she doubtless played her part, dignified, decorative when occasion demanded, in private amusing and witty, must have been much preoccupied with the moon's cycle, for she realized that now everything depended upon her becoming pregnant as soon as possible, carrying the child full-term, and bearing a prince. If she failed in that Henry would find some way of ending this marriage. Even in her most despondent moods she can hardly have visualized the method he would finally take and she could hardly have seen anything threatening in Jane Seymour, so plain of face, prim of manner, and not young, at least thirty.

Jane was the eldest daughter of Sir John Seymour of Wolf Hall in Wiltshire, and Henry had seen her before he halted there on his leisurely progress back from Wales, for Jane had once been one of Katharine's ladies. Not a young woman to catch the eye; indeed unless her portrait maligns her vilely, she may have been the original Plain Jane. Her chin receded and had below it more than a hint of a double chin; her nose was overlarge, a masculine nose; her eyes were slightly protuberant. In her

OPPOSITE Jane Seymour, who replaced Anne as the object of Henry's affections and eventually gave birth to the son Henry longed for

ABOVE Wrought-iron and gilt lock with the arms used by Henry VII and Henry VIII.
From Beddington House, Surrey
OPPOSITE Sketch of jewelry by Holbein

portrait her expression is smug. (She was Queen for so short a time that –
apart from bearing the son Henry craved for – she left little mark, but she
was a kind stepmother to Mary and Elizabeth.)

Two of Jane's brothers, Edward and Thomas, were already at Court,
promising young men in their differing ways, and Henry had little
difficulty in persuading Jane to return to become one of the Queen's
ladies. Because Anne supplanted her mistress, and Jane did the same, there
has been talk of parallel cases and of Nemesis, that Greek goddess who
saw that justice was meted out. But the cases differ. Anne did not return to
Court until *after* Henry's marriage to Katharine had been questioned and
she seems to have tried as far as she was able to avoid confrontations by
having, as soon as possible, an establishment of her own, setting up, as it

were, a separate court. Jane appears to have been less tactful. There is a story of her wearing and ostentatiously fingering a jewel so that Anne asked to see it – Henry's portrait set in diamonds. There is a difference, too, in that Katharine loved Henry and suffered from the loss of his affection. Anne did not love him, and he no longer loved her; but when Jane Seymour returned to Court and in her demure way, flirted with him, King and Queen were again riveted together by the hope of an heir. For in the autumn of 1535, Anne was pregnant again and temporarily, at least, in a strong position; wise enough, experienced enough now not to miscarry – as one story goes – because she chanced to see Jane Seymour on Henry's knee. She would not have risked a miscarriage over such a triviality.

Yet miscarry she did; and those who believed in Nemesis had ample cause to think that she was still active.

Katharine died at Kimbolton on 7 January 1536, and when the news reached London, Anne exclaimed, 'Now I am Queen indeed', and Henry forbade the wearing of any mourning colour, dressing himself in yellow and praising God that now there would be no threat of war from the Emperor. He also ordered a joust to celebrate the occasion; it was to take place at Greenwich on 27 January – the day when Katharine was buried with no more ceremony than was suitable for a Dowager Princess of Wales in Peterborough Cathedral. Henry rode in this tournament, was knocked from the saddle and lay unconscious for two hours.

The Duke of Norfolk, Anne's uncle, but not really her friend, burst in on her and told her that the King was dead. She blamed the subsequent miscarriage on the news, and on the rough way it had been broken to her. She was then, by her own reckoning, three and a half months pregnant and the foetus could be seen to be male.

Henry, restored to consciousness, went into the room where she lay after suffering what was almost a premature birth, and said harshly, 'I see clearly that God does not wish to give me male children.' She tried to explain what had happened. Then he said the fatal words about her getting no more sons by him; and added that he would speak to her when she had recovered.

Whoever said of her that she was braver than a lion was justified then; with her women weeping and wailing all around her, she said that she would conceive again and about the legitimacy of her next son there could be no question, since Katharine was dead.

Brave words; but in another part of the palace Henry was saying that his marriage to Anne had been brought about by witchcraft and that he thought he would take another wife.

And up in Huntingdonshire there was the growing rumour that Katharine had been poisoned. The amateur embalmer, called in hastily, though the weather was cold and no epidemic rife, noticed that her heart was black, not only on the outside, but all through; he had cut it to see. And in her throat there was a lump, also black. Black, poisoned, witchcraft. Nobody seemed to consider that *until* Anne was safely delivered of a son, Katharine was her best defence, since two successive Popes had ordered Henry to leave his concubine and return to his legal wife. Now Katharine was dead and Anne had, as somebody said, 'miscarried of her saviour', and she had no friend, except possibly her brother George who had no real power, and who, in April, was to receive a direct snub. George had been certain of his advancement to a Knight of the Garter, but the honour did not fall to him, it went to Sir Nicholas Carew, no friend of the Boleyn family. The wind of change had veered and was blowing strongly. Henry no longer made any pretence of cohabiting with Anne.

The best she could hope for now was that she should be treated as Katharine had been, her marriage annulled for this reason or that, and herself sent into decent obscurity, bearing perhaps her own, indisputable title of Marquis of Pembroke. A comfortable if deadly dull life. But life...

She cannot possibly have imagined what Henry, that once-loving servitor, signing his letters with a heart, was up to behind her back, and in connivance with Thomas Cromwell. Admittedly he was in a difficult situation; he wanted to get rid of Anne with the least possible waste of time – but on what grounds? Bearing a girl child and then miscarrying three times was not a crime. There had been talk – and was to be more – about a pre-contract with Harry Percy, but both he and Anne had denied its existence. Henry had had more than enough of delay, the very words annulment and divorce were anathema to him, and he did not intend to make another marriage which could be of doubtful validity. The perfect solution would be for Anne to die.

Had she been as Protestant as she is sometimes said to have been, she could have been charged with heresy, but although she showed some interest in books on the subject and had once urged leniency towards a man who, owning such a book, was accused of being a heretic, and

Thomas Cromwell came from the same lower-middle-class background as Wolsey had done but never became a close friend and confidant of the King in the same way as Wolsey had been though, inevitably, she was anti-Papist, in religion she was what Henry was, and what he wished all England to be, Catholic within the Church of England.

While the Spanish Ambassador was writing to the Emperor that the King was already 'as sick and tired of the Concubine as he could be', Cromwell was racking his cunning and unscrupulous mind for a solution to Henry's problem – and, he hoped, the downfall of the whole Boleyn

A contemporary scene of a leg being cauterized. Henry suffered from an incurable sore on his leg and as early medical treatment was crude, his doctors could give Henry little relief from the increasing pain

party. He did much of his best thinking in bed, so he stayed in it for several days, then emerged, a plot already made and ready to be put into action.

It seemed harmless enough on the face of it – a Commission to inquire into any form of treason and to punish the crime. Fisher and More and several others had been executed for one form of treason, but it could take many shapes – down to a quarrel in the yard of an inn where, during an argument of a religious nature, a Catholic of the old kind said to one of the new, 'Then you're a heretic – and the King is another.'

But there was a form of treason which only one person in England could be accused of. In a Queen adultery was treason. Anne must be shown to have committed adultery.

It is likely that when this was first proposed, Henry winced a little – no man likes to clap the cuckold's horns on his own head, and Henry was exceedingly vain and considered himself a good lover. He would, unless the affair were very carefully handled, appear to be the object of ridicule. The woman whom he had wooed for so long, favoured so extravagantly, *loved*, the woman on whose behalf he had broken with the Pope, the woman who – if this charge went ahead – had preferred another man to him! Imagine the nodding heads, the wagging tongues; I told you so! What could he expect?

But if Anne could be made to seem vile enough, so completely given over to lechery that no single man could possibly be expected to satisfy her lust then Henry would attract more sympathy than ridicule. And she could be made to appear so, particularly if incest with her own brother could be quoted as proof of her extreme lasciviousness. It is a measure of Henry's complete revulsion for Anne that he allowed Cromwell to proceed with his scheme, placing spies everywhere, collecting bits of gossip and hearsay.

For a Queen to commit adultery must have been difficult in Tudor times. For everyone privacy was a luxury – and for those who lived in palaces most of all; there were attendants everywhere and most rooms, even sleeping-chambers led into one another. When Henry was hoping to seduce Anne and arranged to have adjoining apartments, he had to have the sentry moved.

There was jousting again at Greenwich on 1 May. Henry was there, but not mentioned among those who took part, which rather confirms the idea that the sore leg was still troubling him. He lent his horse to his friend Sir Henry Norris, who did ride that day, as did Anne's brother. Anne, worried about the future – Henry could hardly bring himself to speak to her now – but with no glimmering of what was in store, watched from a gallery. There was music, but Mark Smeaton did not help to provide it.

He had received an invitation to midday dinner from no less a person than Thomas Cromwell himself. A flattering invitation to a carpenter's son; doubtless he attributed it to his growing reputation as a musician. Clad in his best, he went along through the sunny streets where everybody was keeping the May Day holiday, to Cromwell's house in Stepney. What happened to him as soon as he stepped inside the door there we can never know. One account says that he was 'grievously racked'. But the rack was an instrument of torture not usually found in private houses, and since a fortnight later Smeaton was capable of taking a long walk it seems more likely that the torture was inflicted by materials readily available in any house, a length of knotted cord and a stick. The knotted cord was placed on the victim's head, a circlet just above the eyebrows, tied loosely enough to allow for the insertion of a stick between skull and cord. A twist of the stick and the cord tightened, the knots biting home. It inflicted intense agony, and could interfere with the circulation, causing loss of consciousness; the stick would then be turned in the other direction until consciousness was restored and the suffering wretch would say anything to avoid further agony.

We have – maddeningly – no account of the form this interrogation took. If Cromwell merely asked if Smeaton had anything to confess and Smeaton replied; 'Yes, I have had carnal intercourse with the Queen', it would be far more convincing evidence against her than if, the cord tightening, Cromwell asked; 'Did you ever have carnal intercourse with the Queen?' Say no, and the pain increases; give the answer which is obviously desired and it eases. In such circumstances few men can be heroic, and evidence thus obtained has small value. Mark Smeaton confessed and he involved four other men. Why? To minimize his own guilt? From a smouldering jealousy? Anne herself admitted later that she had given him a snub of the class-conscious kind.

Whatever the answer to these hypothetical questions, Cromwell soon had enough from Mark Smeaton to be able in the afternoon to send Smeaton to the Tower and a messenger to the King at Greenwich.

Henry rose immediately, called upon Sir Henry Norris and a few other of his gentlemen to accompany him and rode away through the flowery fields to London. He left Anne without a word. All unknowing she

OPPOSITE Edward VI, Henry's only son, who was to be succeeded by Mary after his early death

presided over the premature end of the tournament and the dancing which completed the May Day celebrations.

Henry VIII has attracted little sympathy from posterity, but for anybody, even the most heartless, that must have been a terrible ride. And he must have seen all his emotional misery linked with Anne. To strengthen her position as Queen he had passed the Act of Succession, to support that Act he had passed the Act of Supremacy – and killed his best friend, Thomas More. Now, in order to be rid of her, it looked as though he must sacrifice another good friend, Henry Norris, as it had been suggested that he was one of Anne's lovers. Henry managed to edge himself and Norris away from the other riders, told him of what he had been accused, begged him to confess. If only he would, and give information about Anne's other lovers, Norris should go scot-free.

Norris repudiated the whole thing; he said that he was certain of the Queen's innocence and would defend it in single-handed combat, against Henry or any proxy he cared to name. It was the answer of a man of honour; one last echo of what was known as the Age of Chivalry – but then Sir Henry Norris was middle-aged and slightly old-fashioned. The King refused the challenge, and Norris went to the Tower where he was soon joined by Sir Francis Weston who had been made a member of the Order of the Bath at Anne's Coronation, William Brereton, and Lord Rochford, Anne's brother. They all denied the charges and very soon Thomas Wyatt and Sir Richard Page were arrested, but they were released after a short time. Page was banished from Court forever, but Wyatt was taken back into favour and knighted in the following year. No real reason for the difference in their treatment was ever given.

On the morning of 2 May, just as Anne was sitting down to dinner, she was told that some members of the King's Privy Council wished to see her. She went out to receive them and must have seen that their errand was important. There was the Duke of Norfolk, and Thomas Cromwell, and two other officials.

Her uncle, the Duke, upon whose rough manner of breaking the news of Henry's supposed death in January, she blamed that last, fatal miscarriage, now told her, even more roughly, that she was accused of adultery – which was treason – and that Norris and Smeaton, already in the Tower, had confessed. A very old trick, but in this case it did not work. She denied the charge absolutely; she was the King's true wife and

OPPOSITE The Hunt of the Unicorn: the start of the hunt. Henry VIII hunted regularly as he moved from house to house on his summer progresses

Sixteenth-century stoneware jug

no other man had touched her. Norfolk then gave vent to an utterance –
small tribute to his linguistic ability, but so generally agreed upon that it
must be accepted. He said, 'Tut, tut, tut', and shook his head. He was
probably thinking of his own position which must be shored up because it
was shaky; he was the accused woman's uncle and the husband of a
woman who was such a confirmed Katharine supporter that she had
refused to take her place either at the Coronation or at the christening of
Elizabeth. He had no fondness for his niece though while her star was in
the ascendant, he had pretended to be her friend. Now, in order to
establish himself with Henry, he must show her enmity.

   Anne always declared that she was 'cruelly handled' at Greenwich but
there is no proof of physical ill-usage. What she suffered was probably

Oak coffer from Hever Castle carved with the name of Anne's father 'T. Bullen' and the date, 1525

verbal abuse and treatment which, though not violent, indicated that she was no longer to be regarded as Queen. In fact the one man mentioned, and remembered because he treated her with civility, was Sir William Paulet. She was not given an opportunity to change her dress, though there was plenty of time, for traffic on the river always tried to go with the tide. It was at about five o' clock in the afternoon that she made her ironic repetition of her journey from Greenwich to the Tower almost three years earlier. This time no banners, no music, no escort, and her gay, beautifully dressed ladies had been replaced by four women who were either hostile or indifferent.

The dramatic touch which stories need could have been supplied if, this time, she had entered by the well-known Traitors' Gate, that dreaded entrance. Perhaps because there was as yet so little case against her, the barge, silent save for the dipping oars, moved on and stopped at another entrance. There she was met by the man who had welcomed her on the earlier, happy occasion – Sir William Kingston, Constable of the Tower.

To him she said, 'Shall I go into a dungeon?' and he said, 'No, madam, to the lodging that you lay in at your coronation.' It is just possible that this concession, ironic as it seemed, had been organized by Kingston himself. After all his wife was one of the four women appointed to attend – and watch and listen to – Anne day and night and what normal husband would wish to have his wife, because of her appointment, spend hours in dark, damp, underground places?

Lady Kingston was assisted by Lady Boleyn, Anne's aunt by marriage, but no friend, Mistress Stoner and Mistress Coffyn (sometimes spelt Cosyns). They were all ordered to tell her nothing, and only in the presence of Lady Kingston were the others to speak to her at all. Everything Anne said was to be reported to Kingston who would in turn report to Cromwell. Even clear, coherent statements thus transmitted can become strangely twisted and during the first hours in the Tower Anne was anything but coherent. She was suffering from shock. Prepared, ever since January, for something bad to happen to her, she had never foreseen this. So she babbled, as some people do under stress; and although some of her reported statements sound demented, there is sometimes a hidden relevance. It sounds absurd for her to say in the same breath that she had been roughly handled at Greenwich and that her father was hunting at Windsor, yet it sums up her father with precision. His daughter, his son, might be accused of treason and other crimes, but he made no protest. One of the most self-seeking men in a self-seeking age, he took care not to be involved in anything which would lose him favour; and Henry, knowing his man, made no move against him and did not deprive him of any of his offices.

Very different was the behaviour of young Francis Weston's family; as soon as they heard of his arrest on what they were certain was a spurious charge, his parents and his wife rallied to his support and offered the immense sum of 100,000 marks for his life. Ransom money. The Westons must have been as old-fashioned as Sir Henry Norris with his offer of single combat.

Many of Anne's disconnected exclamations have been regarded as proof of her guilt. 'Oh, Norris, hast thou betrayed me?' But she had been told at

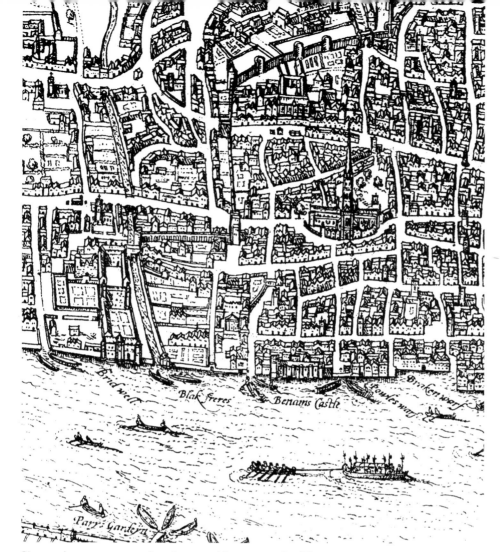

Sixteenth-century map showing royal barges on the Thames

Greenwich that she was accused of adultery and that Norris had confessed to being partner in the crime, and that was a betrayal. She was concerned for her brother; she asked about him and át first Kingston was evasive, but for one accused of treason to be anxious about her kin was a sign of natural, not unnatural, affection. Even calling George her 'sweet brother' was no indication of incest except to those eager to think the worst. It was unfortunate that George, with all his charm, failed to get on with his wife who was so jealous of Anne that she was ready to connive and speak against her husband.

Even in the extremity of pain, Mark Smeaton had not named men at random. All the five accused were those who had stayed faithful and sought Anne's company when others, knowing her to be out of favour, had fallen away. Since January the time-servers, the self-seekers and those with favours to ask had avoided Anne and begun to woo the Seymour faction. Even in gloomy circumstances Anne was capable of being gay in a slightly hysterical manner and the small devoted group – probably with Thomas Wyatt and Richard Page – had made music together, and shared jokes.

And there was this business of courtly love, said to have been introduced into England by Eleanor of Aquitaine, but really far older; a devotion both romantic and Platonic to some lady far out of reach. Looked at against this background the various things reported to have been said, things that were made to sound so deadly, were harmless and understandable.

Consider Henry Norris. He was a widower and the pretty Margaret Shelton, brought to Court by the Boleyns in order to divert Henry's attention from that unnamed lady-about-the-Court, was supposed to be the woman whom he had chosen for his second wife. One day Anne asked him why he did not marry her at once, and he said, 'I will tarry awhile.' Anne replied in the stylized, flirtatious manner of courtly love, 'You look for dead men's shoes? For if aught but good came to the King, you would look to have me.' It was a joke. And Norris replied that if his head ever entertained such a thought it deserved to be cut off.

Consider Francis Weston. Anne twitted him with paying more attention to that same Margaret Shelton than to his wife. He made the inevitable, courtly love answer; there was about the Court one he loved better than all others, 'It is yourself.'

Consider George Boleyn. He had once visited Anne when she was in bed, and he had kissed her, a kiss involving contact of their tongues – what is to this day known as a 'French Kiss' – and to Anne, her formative years spent in France, and to George who had often visited that country, nothing so far out of the ordinary as to mean an incestuous relationship.

Consider Mark Smeaton, on whom so much hinged. One day she had seen him looking sad and asked what was the matter and he said it was of no consequence. But she guessed and said an offensive thing. 'You may not look to have me speak to you as I should do to a nobleman, because you are an inferior person.' She probably meant no more than that he was not qualified to indulge in the meaningless business of courtly love. And he seemed to accept it, saying, 'No, no, Madam. A look sufficeth.'

Anne herself supplied this piece of information which is not incriminating; but *if* she had indeed used him to get herself with child, a great deal can be read into that exchange of words; his resentment at being lover by night and mere musician by day, and her anxiety that he should not presume. But it is all surmise, no more substantial than the hearsay which Cromwell's spies had gathered. Cromwell had hoped for some damning evidence to be given by a maid named Margery, who let him down by denying or retracting everything she had formerly said; and the story of another maid who said she had hidden Mark Smeaton in a wardrobe and let him out when the Queen asked for marmalade to be brought is a slur on Anne's intelligence rather than her morals. Such connivance with a servant would have been dangerous and stupid as well as unnecessary. If Anne wanted music, or anything else, from Mark Smeaton after she had retired, she had only to ask for him and there is some evidence that she did so. However the opportunity to commit an offence is not certain proof that the offence has been committed; it only suggests that it could have been, and it may be that in even considering the possibility, we wrong Anne as much as almost everybody else at the beginning of May 1536 did.

There was presently to be a back-lash of public feeling but when she was first taken to the Tower the mass of the people were delighted. They had never liked her, without quite knowing why; now they knew. She had bewitched the King, poisoned Katharine and indulged her lust with five men, one her brother.

Anne was well aware of her complete isolation and must have compared her plight with that of Katharine who in the darkest days of her humiliation had always had some support, in theory if not in practice, from the Pope, from the Emperor, from men like John Fisher and from the mob of ordinary people. Here shut away in the Tower, guarded by four unfriendly women, visited now and again by Kingston, also unfriendly, though later he was to soften, she must have realized that she was the loneliest woman on earth. In another part of the Tower, Norris, Brereton, Weston and her brother were protesting their innocence – and hers – and in a dungeon, actually in irons as somebody spitefully told her, was Mark Smeaton. She did not hope or expect that any voice from the outer world would be raised in her defence.

But one was, and it was, surprisingly, that of Thomas Cranmer.

IO

The Last Days

The people will have no difficulty in finding a nickname, for me.
I shall be Queen Anne Lackhead.

Anne Boleyn

Thomas Cranmer is best remembered as a turncoat, the man who
recanted, and then, recanting upon his recantation, was condemned to be
burnt as a heretic. As the flames mounted, he thrust out his right hand –
the one that had signed the recantation – into the fire, saying that having
done the signing, it should be first to be burned.

In fact he was a man, capable, like most men, not of steadfast courage,
but flashes of bravery every now and then. He had one such flash on 3
May, the day after Anne had been taken to the Tower. In that same right
hand he took up his pen and wrote to Henry. He knew that he owed his
elevation from humble tutor to Archbishop of Canterbury to the situation
which Henry's infatuation for Anne had brought about; he knew all the
Boleyn family well, and before he took Holy Orders, he had been married
for a short time; he may have known rather more about women than a
totally celibate priest could have done. He was deeply shocked and
surprised by the news of Anne's arrest and by the nature of the charges
brought against her.

'I am in such perplexity that my mind is clean amazed; for I never had
better opinion in women than I had in her, ' he wrote, 'which maketh me
think she should not be culpable.' One imagines the pen halting there and
the perplexed mind asking itself: Too strongly worded? Likely to offend?
He wrote on, hastily, 'And again, I think that Your Highness would not
have gone so far, except she had surely been culpable.' The well-meant,
slightly schizophrenic letter went on to say that Cranmer hoped Anne

OPPOSITE In 1537 Henry VIII commissioned Holbein to paint a mural on the wall of
the Privy Chamber at Whitehall depicting himself with his father, Henry VII, in the
background. It also included Jane Seymour

Richmond Palace in 1562 drawn by the Dutch artist Anthony van Wyngaerde

would be able to prove her innocence, or that if she could not, the King would be merciful.

Cranmer had been associated with Henry long enough to know that mercy was not one of his outstanding qualities. Henry had changed from the time when, returning from war in France, he had found the body of his enemy, the King of Scots, defeated at Flodden, thrown like rubbish into an attic, and given it a decent, even honourable burial in Westminster Abbey. Yet Cranmer's confused letter may not have been completely wasted, for in the end Henry was to show Anne as much mercy as was consistent with the sentence passed upon her.

Henry's attitude towards the whole business was a pretended ignorance and aloofness; he, too, seemed surprised and shocked. That colloquy with Cromwell might never have taken place, that order for action against treason in any form, worded so generally, yet with Anne as its target, might never have been signed. All day Henry went about wearing the look of a man who had been grossly betrayed. He said he was ready to believe that more than a hundred men had had intercourse with Anne, and he laid special emphasis on crimes other than adultery. Weeping, he told the young Duke of Richmond that he and Mary were fortunate to be alive since 'that accursed whore' had determined to poison them, and he said that harm had been done to his own body. This was most likely a reference to the leg injury which had ulcerated and would not heal. Yet it was only five months since Anne had enjoyed, because of her pregnancy, the precarious renewal of favour, and never once had Henry questioned the paternity of the child; on the contrary he had often referred to 'my boy'.

In the evening, the mood changed; in his gayest clothes, and to the sound of music, Henry had himself rowed seven miles up-river to the house of Sir Nicholas Carew where Jane Seymour was staying, well out of range of talk about such nasty things as adultery and incest. Supping and making merry, joyfully looking forward to his third marriage, Henry seemed not to have a care in the world. As Chapuys wrote, 'You never saw prince or other man who displayed his horns more or wore them more gladly.' Other people learned about these nightly junketings and there began a slow swing of public opinion in Anne's favour.

Henry had been careful of Jane's reputation as he had never been of Anne's. He had given her his portrait set in diamonds, it is possible that he had once or twice fondled her openly. But Jane had the advantage of having a brother, Edward, who had been close to the King during his wooing of Anne, and had seen how Henry's desire to possess was always spurred by resistance. So presently Jane was only having private talk with Henry in Edward's own apartments and under Edward's eye; and she began to refuse presents, saying that she must not do anything to endanger her reputation for virtue since she hoped to make a good marriage and had only her good name as dowry.

Kingston who had been Constable of the Tower for some years, said that he had never seen a prisoner like Anne. He was probably right; the variability of mood, the speech, now flippant, now serious, all the things which had held Henry entranced for so long, were still in evidence. 'For one hour she is determined to die, and the next hour to the contrary', the bewildered Kingston wrote. Some of her talk was disjointed and some indiscreet as when she said, 'I fear Weston most', though at his trial this cryptic remark was explained – she had lent him money, a fact that could be twisted. Yet the letter she wrote to Henry, 'from my doleful prison in the Tower', was a model of dignity, restraint and concern, not for herself, but for others. She, like Cranmer, had seen how Henry dealt with those who opposed him. So she did not ask for mercy, merely justice, that she should be given a fair trial and not be judged by her enemies. She did ask for mercy to be shown to the poor innocent gentlemen accused with her and she begged Henry not to let 'that stain – that unworthy stain of a disloyal heart towards your good Grace ever cast so foul a blot on me, or on the infant Princess, your daughter.'

This letter may well have had the very opposite effect than that intended. It reminded Henry of Elizabeth's existence and of the fact that by the Act of Succession she was declared legitimate and heir – failing a brother – to the throne. About that something must be done and he was prepared to do it – with Cranmer's help. The Succession had always been of vital importance to him, and his one recorded testy remark made to Jane Seymour concerned it. She was talking about what she meant to do for Mary and Elizabeth once she was Queen, and Henry told her, rather harshly, that she should rather think about her own children, fathered by him, children who – with Katharine dead, and Anne dead, and both his former marriages disallowed, would have indisputable claim to the throne. And pray God, at last a living boy. (That dream did come true. Jane in October 1537 gave birth to the Prince whom Henry had wanted ever since his marriage to Katharine in 1509. Jane died of puerperal fever, made worse by the hustling about during the christening celebrations.) But when Anne said that if Henry condemned her, she hoped God would pardon him, she was expressing a wish which was not to be wholly fulfilled. Out of all the horrendous muddle, involving six marriages, Henry, when he died in 1547, left just the one frail boy, not yet a full ten years old, and two daughters, both in their turn declared illegitimate, Mary, aged thirty-one, Elizabeth, fourteen. And that he was obliged to mention his two daughters in his will was proof of defeat, and showed that though God may have pardoned him, it was not to the extent of blessing him with two or three sturdy boys.

Perhaps Cromwell, preparing the indictment against Anne, had hoped that Norris, Weston, Brereton and George Boleyn would confess, as Smeaton had done, thus making the trial a mere formality. That would explain why the charges were so sloppily drawn up, accusing Anne of committing adultery with Henry Norris rather less than a month after Elizabeth's birth, a time when even the most raging nymphomania might be thought to be inactive. Another date given was when she was pregnant and hopeful again, a time when, by sixteenth-century belief, sexual intercourse was a direct invitation to miscarry. Another date was misaligned, too. Anne and her brother George were said to have planned the King's death while Katharine of Aragon was still alive, and with Henry dead, leaving no heir but Mary, their future would have been gloomy and possibly short.

If the four accused men had confessed, or even weakened, Cromwell's task would have been made easier; but they all denied the charges and went on stalwartly protesting their innocence and, therefore, the Queen's. And their behaviour should not be set in contrast with poor Mark Smeaton's; he had been tortured, they were not. The Tudor class structure was very rigid; when all five men were in the Tower, charged with the same offence, only Smeaton was in a dungeon, 'in irons' as Mrs Stoner told Anne maliciously, hoping to see her wince. Anne, knowing her world, said, 'That is because he is no gentleman. But he was never in my chamber but at Winchester and there I sent for him to play the virginals, for there my chamber was above the King's.'

Another slightly irrelevant statement, but in context it made sense. Henry would have heard the music stop.

Since the offences were said to have taken place in Middlesex and in Kent, juries, the twelve good men and true, for so long the representatives of law and justice, were called to meet at Westminster and at Deptford. As the law then ran, a man was assumed guilty until proved innocent and all these first jurymen had to do was to decide whether the evidence given justified the passing of the charge to a higher court. Both assemblies of jurymen decided that a true bill had been presented, and on 12 March the four commoners – Norris, Weston, Brereton and Smeaton, were marched through the streets to Westminster Hall to be tried.

Mark Smeaton again pleaded guilty – he could hardly do otherwise; the other three denied all charges, and this time the jury considered its verdict under the eyes of some of the King's Commissioners, including – incredibly – the Earl of Wiltshire, Anne's father, anxious, over-anxious, to show that whatever happened to his son and daughter, he was loyal to the King. The verdict was inevitable; all four were condemned to die, to be beheaded by the axe on Tower Green.

There is the usual controversy about this sentence; some writers say that Mark Smeaton, because he was the most common of the commoners, was hanged, drawn and quartered at Tyburn but what little blurred and confused evidence that there is, rather indicates that though he was not a gentleman, in the end he was treated as one, and shared the fate of the others. A good death, or a bad one, depending upon the strength and skill of the man who wielded the axe. It could be a swift, if bloody death, or it could be, as was shown in 1541 when the old Lady Salisbury went to the block, a clumsy, hacking butchery.

Anne and her brother, because they had been ennobled, must be tried

Judges in their robes. The trial of the accused men was held in Westminster Hall

by their peers. Cromwell thought it unwise to take them through the streets to Westminster for the well-known English sympathy with the underdog had now surfaced and there might be riots in the street, or even an attempt at rescue. At her zenith Anne had been hated, now she was pitied, and the badly drawn indictment, the staunch denial of the three men tried on the day before had predisposed people in her favour. As for George Boleyn, belief in his innocence was so strong that men were betting ten to one that he would be acquitted. It was not that incest was so rare and unnatural a thing as to be unbelievable; everybody knew it happened, but in overcrowded hovels with brothers and sisters sharing a bed, among people whose lives were so isolated, or their appearance so unattractive, as to make normal sexual contact difficult. That two young, attractive people, both married, both with ample choice of other partners, should resort to incest seemed, to say the least, unlikely.

A room within the Tower precincts had been fitted out as a court. The Duke of Norfolk, as the King's representative and judge, sat under a canopy and the twenty-six selected peers took their places. Anne's father, Lord Wiltshire, had expressed his willingness to serve, but a belated sense of nicety on somebody's part had caused this offer to be refused. The Earl of Northumberland was there, however, though he was a very sick man.

He probably thought that Anne stood a chance of being acquitted, for on the previous day he had been visited by a friend, sent by Cromwell to persuade him to agree that he had been betrothed to Anne and that, therefore, her marriage to the King had never been legal. The resurrection of this old question rather hinted that Henry was willing to get rid of Anne without having her executed for treason. It must have put Northumberland in a painful position. He had once, in a temper, flung the pre-contract with Anne at his wife; but at a solemn inquiry into the matter he had denied that there had ever been such a pre-contract. And he now stuck to that denial. If the King wanted to end this marriage on a legal quibble, he had another to fall back upon – the consanguinity argument, Mary Boleyn having been Henry's mistress. One may be reasonably sure that Northumberland had followed the career of his lost love with close attention and knew every detail. What he could not have known was that Henry's wish to prove this marriage null and void did not arise from his wish to spare Anne, but from a desire to bastardize Elizabeth whom he had legitimized by the Act of Succession. For suppose Jane Seymour had no child. Suppose – and what a deadly supposition! – that Henry's impotence, a thing whispered about, should prove to be fact.

Behind the peers, representing the people, but having no voice in the verdict – were the Lord Mayor and the Aldermen of the City of London, and the Heads of the principal Guilds, many of whom, on another May day almost, not quite, three years earlier had, with music and banners, escorted Anne on her river journey from Greenwich to the Tower.

A chair on a platform had been prepared for Anne; when all was ready, Sir William Kingston brought her to it with Lady Kingston and Lady Boleyn in attendance. Grace and style, rather than mere prettiness, had always been her assets, and now even those who hated her noted her dignity. 'She made an entry as though she were going to a great triumph and sat down with elegance.'

She had always been, essentially, a woman dependent upon herself. Alone, miserable and heart-broken at Hever long ago, she had managed the difficult business of enticing Henry with one hand, repelling him with the other – but she had attained her aim, she had been anointed and crowned Queen of England. Now and again over the years, something within her, like the over-strung string of a viol, had cracked and she had given way to temper, hysteria, even to over-optimism, as when she said that she thought the King had sent her to the Tower merely to try her. But now, dependent upon no one but herself, knowing that four men, one making a confession that damned her, three professing their innocence – and hers – lay in the Tower, condemned and awaiting death, she knew she had nothing to rely upon except herself. And she did not let herself down.

She listened, apparently unmoved by anger, shame or embarrassment, to the monstrous charges brought against her. No witnesses were called; the rumour that the Queen had been found in bed with her organist was not substantiated by the evidence of anyone who had seen Mark Smeaton in her bed. The prosecution had no witnesses, nor had the defence. Here she was alone again. In her own defence she spoke soberly and briefly, denying all the charges brought against her. She had, she admitted, given Sir Henry Norris a trinket or two, and lent Sir Francis Weston some money; she had danced with men, but she had never committed adultery.

And it seems to have occurred to nobody – not even to Anne herself – that if in his roundabout way Henry was trying to prove that Anne had never been his legal wife, then the charge of treason now brought against her, lost its final sting. Only adultery by a Queen ranked as treason, and if she had never been Queen, she could not be condemned to die.

Curiously, nobody stood up and said this. On the previous day the Earl of Northumberland had been asked to make a statement which would have shown that Anne had never been Queen of England, never Henry's wife and, therefore, she could have slept with those hundred mythical men without committing a capital crime.

The peers cast their votes, beginning with the youngest. Guilty, guilty, guilty. When it came to Northumberland's turn, he said the same, for

OPPOSITE Thomas Howard, 3rd Duke of Norfolk by Holbein. Although the Duke was Anne's uncle, it was he who told Anne roughly that she was accused of adultery and must go to the Tower

S. Iemes Parke

Charing crosse

The Courte gate

The Courte

Preuy bridge

Kinges ftreate

Chanor row

Westmynster hall

Starre Chamber

...mynster

The olde Palace

The Quee..nts bridge

The lambeth

what could one dissentient voice do against twenty-five? But having cast his vote, he was so overcome by bodily weakness and by emotion that he collapsed, and though taken out, lain by an open window, and given the rough-and-ready restoratives of the day, he could take no part in the trial of George Boleyn which began immediately after the Duke of Norfolk had pronounced sentence upon Anne. 'Thou hast deserved death and thy judgment is this: That thou shalt be burnt here within the Tower of London on the Green, else to have thy head smitten off as the King's pleasure shall be further known.'

In the hush that followed this pronouncement, Anne was heard to say, 'Oh God, thou knowest if I have merited this death.' Then, with no sign of the hysteria which had marked her first hours in the Tower, she addressed her judges. 'I think you know well the reason why you have condemned me to be other than that which led you to this judgment. My only sin against the King has been my jealousy and lack of humility. But I am prepared to die. What I regret most deeply is that men who were innocent and loyal to the King must lose their lives because of me.' In that speech there is a touch of the asperity which Henry had once so greatly dreaded.

That she was being victimized was an opinion shared by many, including the Lord Mayor of London, who as a magistrate was accustomed to weighing evidence, for and against. He said, 'I could not see anything in the proceeding against her, but that they were resolved to make an occasion to get rid of her.'

And even Chapuys, for so long her enemy because he was Katharine's friend and Mary's, said that he thought Anne deserved better treatment than she received.

As she was led away, her brother took her place. He was charged with a medley of offences, incest, plotting the King's death, making mock of the King generally, his clothing, his literary pretensions, and ...

If only George could have kept his mouth shut and refrained from the final mockery, he might have been spared and several honest citizens could have collected on their wagers. The last accusation was something that must not be spoken about even in a life-and-death trial. Nobody was prepared to stand up and ask him if on a given date his wife had told him that the Queen had said that the King was impotent. He was told to read

Agas's map of London, showing how important the Thames was as a transport route, especially for barges

the question and answer 'Yes' or 'No'. Something reckless and defiant rose up in George Boleyn, and something of vengeance, too. He knew – who better? – how the sister he loved had been treated, and the temptation to administer a last prick to Henry's vanity was too strong to be resisted. He read the forbidden question aloud and all his peers who, having condemned Anne, thus doing what was asked of them, and having been severe with her might have been disposed to be lenient with him, declared him guilty and the Duke of Norfolk sentenced him to the worst death of all; he was to be dragged to Tyburn, hanged, cut down, 'his members cut off and his bowels taken out of his body and burnt before him.' Then his head was to be cut off and his body quartered and his head and pieces of his body, 'to be set at such places as the King should assign.'

The worst death that the law could inflict. One would have thought that even Henry, growing more and more insensitive over the years, would have been satisfied. And had he been simply the brutal tyrant, the bloodthirsty Bluebeard of fiction, he would have allowed Anne to burn and George to suffer as the Carthusians had done.

One wonders why neither extreme penalty was ever exacted.

Why?

Every birth is a death sentence. This is common knowledge though most people prefer not to accept it. Even people who have lived an ordinary, full life and are stricken, hope for a palliative dose, a miracle, a few more days. Only those who know that death must come on a certain calendar date, can possibly understand the feelings of Anne and her five so-called 'paramours' at this time.

What the others felt, how they thought, we cannot tell; Anne and George, both gifted, found refuge in the making of verses.

Anne tuned her lute and fitted words to the sad tune:

> Oh death rock me asleep,
> Bring on my quiet rest,
> Let pass my very guiltless ghost
> Out of my careful breast.
> Ring out the doleful knell,
> Let its sound my death tell;
> For I must die,
> There is no remedy,
> For now I die ...

There were two more verses, all sounding the same note of hopeless resignation; and indeed Kingston, her gaoler, reported that she faced

Anne Boleyn's lute. An accomplished lute player, Anne accompanied herself when she sang her own songs

death in a way surprising to him who had seen so many men, and women too, executed. 'This lady hath much pleasure and joy in death,' he wrote.

But another set of verses reveals a slightly different frame of mind.

> Defiled is my name, full sore
> Through cruel spite and false report,
> That I may say for evermore,
> Farewell to joy, adieu comfort.
> For wrongfully you judge of me
> Unto my fame a mortal wound,
> Say what ye list, it may not be,
> Ye seek for that shall not be found.

She minded, not death but the infamy.

George Boleyn's last verses are better known, less personal, perhaps of more literary merit.

> Farewell my lute, this is the last
> Labour that thou and I shall waste,
> For ended is that we began,
> Now is the song both sung and past.
> My lute be still, for I have done.

Before Anne could go to her 'quiet rest', more was required of her. Henry VIII might be, as she had once said, a prey to light fancies but his concern about the Succession was genuine enough. It was fundamentally Katharine's failure to give him an heir which had started the whole imbroglio. Anne had failed, too. Would Jane? Quite possibly he had doubts about his own potency and if so they would have been inflamed by the things, true or false, which Anne was reported to have said to her brother in jest; but there was an axiom about the truth of things said in jest. Now, on the verge of his third marriage, Henry looked back and took stock. If he failed Jane, or Jane failed him, he would leave Mary, declared illegitimate by Cranmer's court at Dunstable, Elizabeth by reference to that same court's decision, legitimate, and by Act of Parliament made heir to the throne unless she had a brother. Elizabeth was not quite three years old. The idea of being succeeded by a child – and the child of a disgraced mother – would have appalled any man.

More and more Henry's mind turned to the young Duke of Richmond, now fourteen years old and by Tudor standards, on the verge of manhood. He was a promising boy, accepted by everyone as Henry's son and nobody had objected when in a single ceremony Henry had knighted him, then made him Duke of Richmond – the title held by Henry's father before he took the throne – made him Lord Admiral of England and bestowed upon him many other titles appertaining to lands in France now lost, but not forgotten. The only bar to his peaceful succession to the throne was his illegitimacy. If Elizabeth could be made to seem illegitimate, too, then in the event of Henry's dying without any other children, he would leave three bastards and the boy would succeed simply by virtue of his sex. Anne must somehow be persuaded to admit that her marriage was no marriage.

One of the most diligent researchers into this story regrets that there is so little documentation. In the absence of it conflicting stories arose and the obscurity which shrouded Anne's early life, thickens towards the end. She had an interview with Cranmer, that is certain, but one account says that she was taken under cover of darkness to Lambeth Palace where Cranmer received her in a low close room. Another says that Cranmer came to the Tower and that seems slightly more likely. The fear of an attempted rescue was growing. It had been considered unwise to take her to Westminster for trial, in full daylight, with an escort of the Yeomen of the Guard. A night journey would be equally risky; and since the ostensible reason for Anne and Cranmer to spend some time alone together was that he should hear her confession and give her absolution, it would be more in keeping with custom for confessor to visit prisoner than for the prisoner to go out to the confessor.

Cranmer was now in a more embarrassing situation than Clement had been when asked to declare Henry's marriage to Katharine void. Clement had merely to reverse a decision made by his predecessor; Cranmer was asked to reverse his own judgment, given only three years earlier. Yet he dared not offend Henry, and it is possible that he saw in his secret orders a chance to do Anne – and her brother – some small service. Everything in Cranmer's record indicates that though pliable, he was kindly; he had been closely associated with the Boleyn family, and pretend as he might, could not believe Anne and George guilty. Also, with his trained mind, he may have seen that if Anne could be coaxed into admitting that her marriage had never existed, then even if she had committed adultery, she should not die as a traitor.

Nobody now can know what was said at this meeting between the Queen and the Archbishop whose lives had been so closely entwined. Did Cranmer, as one writer suggests, deny her absolution until she gave way, or did he promise, and this seems more likely, some reprieve, some mitigation of the cruel deaths to which she and George were condemned? It was all very secret.

Anne had been almost as stubborn as Katharine had been in holding that her marriage was sound, her child both royal and legitimate. When the pre-contract with Harry Percy had come up, she had denied it, and so had he, more than once. There remained the consanguinity – though, strictly speaking, that was no more a bar to legitimate marriage now in May 1536 than it had been in January 1533 when she and Henry had been married, or in June of the same year when she had been crowned. Nothing had changed except Henry's fancy.

Cranmer went away satisfied; next morning at Lambeth, in another collusive gathering not unlike that court at Dunstable, he was able to declare that Henry's marriage to Anne was no more valid than Henry's marriage to Katharine and the daughter of this marriage was as illegitimate as Mary. (Elizabeth was, in a precocious age, the most precocious; informed of her change in status, she said, 'How haps it? Yesterday my lady Princess and today but my Lady Elizabeth?')

Out of the mists of speculation and hazard, two facts loom and they may be concerned with Anne's talk with Cranmer; she was not burned but she was beheaded in the most merciful way then known; and her brother did not suffer the long-drawn torturing death to which he had been condemned. He was, like the other accused, simply beheaded. One cannot but suspect that some kind of bargain had been struck during that so secret meeting. There is no other apparent reason for the mitigation of George Boleyn's fate; the King was not likely to show mercy to a man who had mocked his impotency and spoken the horrible word in public.

Anne seems to have thought, for a brief time, that her life was to be spared; to the women who watched and guarded her, she spoke of the possibility of her sentence being commuted into banishment – she thought to Antwerp. If she believed that, she was, for about the first time, deluding herself. Henry had married her while another woman, claiming to be his wife, was still alive. He wanted no repetition of that. Anne must die, but with a swift certainty, by one stroke of the headsman brought over from Calais, the town which, though still English, was French in its culture and where heads fell under the sword, not the axe.

OPPOSITE Thomas Cromwell replaced Wolsey as Henry's adviser and chief minister
OVERLEAF *Fête at Bermondsey* by Joris Hoefnagel. Although this was painted in 1570, it shows how rural London was even then, with the Tower of London and the Thames in the background

Her so-called 'paramours' were to die first. And here again is confusion. It adds poignancy to Anne's story to say that part of her torture during her last days was to watch them go. Five men, all but Norris young and one her brother, who were to lose their lives, as she had said at her trial, because of her. There are quite moving accounts of how she watched the heads struck off, the life-blood spouting. But Tower Green, where the men were to suffer, and the Royal apartments where Anne was housed were not within sight of each other. So we must fall back on compromise, on an account that says that she was led to a window overlooking the place of execution. If so, did she watch with the fascination of horror, or turn away, shuddering and sickened?

The four men who had denied the sin of adultery, did not confess on the scaffold. That was significant for the Tudor Age was a time of belief. Men might differ about ritual, about who was Head of the Church, but there were few agnostics or atheists. George Boleyn, Francis Weston, Henry Norris and William Brereton all believed that when their heads were struck off, their souls would face God and His Judgment. To die with a lie upon your lips, or a sin unconfessed was to invite a punishment far more severe than any man could inflict; yet not one of them cleared his conscience by making a last-minute confession. This – strong evidence in Anne's favour – meant far more in the sixteenth century than it does today, unless taken in context.

But alongside the matter of a man, his immortal soul and the judgment awaiting him, there were a few mundane considerations. Condemned men were expected to admit that they deserved the sentence imposed upon them by their worldly judges. Failure to do so was a criticism of the law of the land, of the authority that had condemned them – and that could be looked upon as another form of treason which could lead to the forfeiture of all the dead man's property, and the persecution of his family. So nauseatingly sycophantic speeches were often made from the scaffold in order to protect a few acres, a few hoarded coins, or the safety of those about to be bereaved.

George Boleyn died first, and so bravely that he was said to have set an example to the others. Like the others, he confessed to general sinfulness and he put in a word for the new, Reformed religion. But he did not

ABOVE A stained-glass window at Hever Castle showing the arms of Henry VIII flanked by those of Anne Boleyn and Anne of Cleves
BELOW Embarkation of Henry VIII for Boulogne, 1520. Dover Castle is in the top left-hand corner and the ships' streamers fly the Tudor colours of green and white

incriminate Anne, nor did any of the others. Sir Henry Norris made no speech; Sir Francis Weston was cryptic, 'I had thought to live in abomination yet this twenty or thirty years and then to have made amends. I thought little it would come to this.' William Brereton said, 'I have deserved to die, were it a thousand deaths. But the cause for which I die, judge ye not, but if ye judge, judge the best.' Mark Smeaton, who had confessed, knew that to withdraw now might mean that he would be snatched away and killed more slowly and painfully, so he simply said, 'Masters, I pray you all pray for me, for I have deserved the death.'

The public was admitted to executions and as a rule the scaffold was set high so that even those on the fringe of the crowd could see and be warned, or entertained, for an execution ranked with the brutal sports – bull-, bear- and horse-baiting, dogfights, cockfights – in which the people delighted. They brought their children to watch, and food to eat within sight of the gory spectacle. It was an outing, and if the person who suffered happened to be unpopular the mob made its feelings known.

On this 17 May there was something about the crowd's behaviour which made the authorities think about tomorrow, the day fixed for

OPPOSITE Robert Cheseman, the King's falconer, by Holbein
BELOW Lambeth Palace where Henry's marriage to Anne was declared invalid and their daughter, Elizabeth, illegitimate

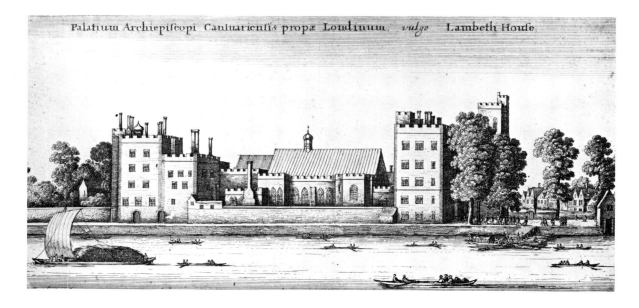

Palatium Archiepiscopi Cantuariensis propa Londinum, *vulgo* Lambeth House.

ROBERTVS CHESEMAN .
ANNO . DM .

ÆTATIS . SVÆ . XLVIII ·
M · D · XXXIII ·

Anne's execution. A lower scaffold so that people saw less, and then – brilliant idea – an alteration of the time; let it be postponed, so that people grew tired of waiting. Changed from the morning of the 18th, to the afternoon, her execution was at last deferred until the 19th.

The five men had died as traitors, but there is no mention of their heads being exposed on spikes. There was a general agreement that the less made of this the better. The bodies were hastily put into 'shells', a word that implies that they were not ordinary coffins, and as hastily buried within the precincts of the Tower.

Een Grave oft Lord
van den Parlemente

Een Lord van
der ordre, zoo sy
ghecleedt
gaen op St.
Gooris dach.

Eenen
rider Alages

II

Anne's Execution

Finish, good lady, the bright day is done,
And we are for the dark.

ANTHONY AND CLEOPATRA: *Shakespeare*

There is internal, if not external, evidence that two of Anne's friends, Margaret Lee and another woman had been allowed to come into the Tower, though they were not allowed to talk to her privately and were housed in distant apartments. If they were there it was probably a concession by Kingston whose attitude towards his extraordinary prisoner had softened considerably. Required by Cromwell to watch her closely and report every trivial thing, the Constable had moved from hostility, to curiosity, to unwilling admiration and then to pity. When, hearing that her execution had been postponed, she exclaimed that she was sorry, since she had hoped by that time to be dead and past her pain; he did his best to comfort her by saying there would be no pain, it was so subtle. And she said, 'I have heard say that the executioner is very good. And I have a little neck.' She put her hand to it and laughed. One wonders – since nobody was supposed to tell her anything, how she had heard about the skilled headsman – a highly paid man who for one minute's work charged £23 6s 8d., quite apart from the cost of his fare from Calais, and home again.

She laughed when she spoke of her slim neck, always such a noticeable feature, but on the whole her mood was sombre for she, too, was about to face God and His Judgment. She asked Kingston to share the Last Sacrament with her and her women – one can only hope that her two friends were allowed to be present also. She wanted, for the last time, to declare her innocence.

One of the things upon which Catholics and Protestants were to split was the matter of Transubstantiation; at the moment when the priest

OPPOSITE Two peers in their robes with their halberdier

blessed the wafer, or the bread, and the wine, did they become the very body and blood of Christ, or was the whole thing symbolic, though no less a solemnity? Anne may have been interested in the new Reformed religion, but she was a Catholic still and in this last solemn ceremony taking the body of Christ into her mouth, she said, 'I am innocent.'

And this does not entirely refute the supposition – the guess – the near-possibility of her resort, in desperation, to Mark Smeaton. In that so-secret meeting with Cranmer, alongside the bargaining, she could have confessed, been set some penance and absolved. A sin thus cancelled out need not be confessed again. And of the concocted charges which she had always denied, she could say in good faith, 'I am innocent.'

There is, of course, just another possibility – that she was in fact the witch that Henry said she was; that she had gone over to the Devil, been given *almost* everything she wanted, even the Crown, and then, since this was Satan's habit, been callously abandoned. In that case taking the Sacrament and telling a lie at the same time, could have been one more tribute to her dark master, offered perhaps in the hope of some magical aid even at the eleventh hour. (It is a matter of history that some witches did die with exceptional courage and defiance. It is also fact that witchcraft tended to extend from mother to daughter and that Anne's daughter, the great Elizabeth, if she did not directly dabble in black magic, believed in it, and actually allowed a notorious occultist to choose the date of her Coronation. These may be idle thoughts, but are not presented frivolously.)

One thing which troubled Anne during her last hours was her treatment of Princess Mary. We have only Lady Kingston's account of the dramatic scene when Anne asked her to sit in the Queen's chair and went down on her knees – asking Lady Kingston to do the same when she saw Mary – and asked her to forgive her.

If she had indeed plotted, as she said, against Mary's life, the plots had been singularly ineffectual. Mary's health was precarious, separation from her mother, the rejection of her father, the uncertainty of her whole future was not conducive to good health. Chapuys, so watchful, would certainly have reported any attempt to poison or assassinate Mary. He never did. And the ill-treatment which finally broke Mary's proud spirit did not begin until Anne had gone to her grave.

OPPOSITE Anne Boleyn's gateway at Hampton Court with an astronomical clock by Nicholas Oursian

Rood screen at King's College Chapel, Cambridge showing Henry VIII's and Anne Boleyn's initials intertwined. Jeers of 'HA HA' were heard in protest against them

So perhaps Anne exaggerated, or gave way to neurotic feelings of guilt, remembering things spoken in anger when her overtures were rejected. Or perhaps she was as forward-looking, as far-planning as she had been ten years ago – what a vast span of time – at Hever.

Tomorrow she would die; and by her own admission, extracted only God and Cranmer knew under what duress, she had slapped the label 'bastard' on to her own child. And who would care for that child or have power to protect her? Certainly no member of the Boleyn family, certainly not the King. But there was Mary Tudor, tried, tested, resolute, and still, for many people in England and most on the Continent, heir to the throne. If Henry failed in his third marriage – and of all the people at that moment, Anne had best reason to suspect that he would – then Mary would be Queen. So Anne knelt and sent sycophantic messages and Lady Kingston, saying that she had often played the fool in her youth and was prepared to do it again, went through the masquerade. And Mary accepted the oblique apology and the responsibility. She was at an age when she should have had a child of her own and Elizabeth was an engaging little girl; the love-hate relationship between them had already begun and was to last until Mary, on her deathbed, sent to Elizabeth the Queen's Jewels and gave England into her care.

Now the last day dawned and brightened. Anne, always stylish where clothes were concerned, rose and dressed herself for the last time in damask – all the accounts agree upon that, but some say black, some say grey. Whatever the colour it was set off by a wide white collar. The famous wealth of black hair was neatly coiled up – hanging free it could have impeded the swift cut of the sword. What was perched upon it? A hood of black velvet, crusted with pearls, a small hat with a coif, or the wide, bugled one which her statue at Blickling wears? One story says one thing, one another. The sleepless nights, the tears, the grief for the dead, seem not to have impaired her appearance. One observer remarked that he had never seen her look more beautiful. This was the last scene she was to play in life and she faced it with the old courage and dignity.

Before she stepped out into the sunshine for the last time she sent Henry a message, so scathing that no one dared deliver it. An undelivered, verbal message might be of doubtful authenticity, but this one was so typical of Anne that it could hardly have been invented. 'Commend me to His Majesty and tell him that he hath ever been constant in his career of advancing me; from a private gentlewoman he made me a Marchioness, from a Marchioness a Queen and now that hath left no higher degree of honour he gives my innocency the crown of martyrdom.'

The authorities had ordered that no foreigner was to be present in the Tower; that rule had been obeyed, but the ruse of changing the time, even the date of the execution had not worked; the space was crowded, the mood of the crowd again subdued.

Kingston led Anne to the steps which led to the unusually low scaffold; one account says that he helped her to mount them, another says that she did so unaided. From the low eminence she looked down upon her last audience, those who had come to see her die. Neither her father nor her uncle was there. Charles Brandon, Duke of Suffolk, was. One can imagine how avidly he had listened to the stories of the King's loss of manhood and of Elizabeth being declared illegitimate. If Henry died leaving only three bastards, the chance of the Crown passing to the daughter of Charles

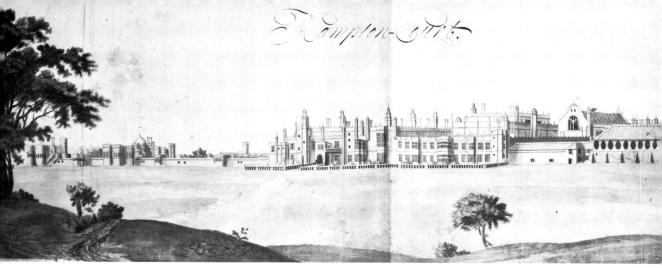

Henry married Jane Seymour at Hampton Court a few days after Anne was beheaded

Brandon and the King's sister would be greatly enhanced. The young Duke of Richmond was there, possibly already showing signs of the disease that was to claim him within a year. Thomas Cromwell had come to watch the *dénouement* of his plot, and the last thought in his mind, at this moment of triumph, would have been that four years later he would be standing where Anne now stood. There were other important people, among them the Lord Mayor who believed that Anne was innocent.

The headsman from Calais stood a little to one side, his sword, so heavy that it needed both hands to wield it, sharp and bright in the sunshine.

Anne made the routine speech; 'Good Christian people, I am come hither to die, according to the law, for by the law I am judged to die, and therefore I will speak nothing against it.' Her next words may have been dictated by the thought of Elizabeth whose future was so dependent upon Henry, or they may have been delivered with all the sarcasm of which Anne was capable. Something about the words or the way in which they were spoken, or the way in which they were received made a mark and when, six years later, Anne's cousin, Catherine Howard, was beheaded in this place for the same reason though with rather more justification, she was forbidden to address the crowd *because* of what Anne had said.

Yet the words seem harmless enough. 'But I pray God save the King and send him long to reign over you. For a gentler nor a more merciful prince was there never; and to me he was ever a good, a gentle and sovereign lord. And if any person will meddle of my cause I require them to judge the best. And thus I take my leave of the world and of you all, and I heartily desire you all to pray for me.'

Four women were in attendance; they were not named so one may have been the devoted Margaret Lee. There is still in existence a small book of devotions, bound in gold and black enamel, said to have been given by

Anne to Margaret during her last moments. But Anne herself removed her head-dress and the collar. She knelt, said, 'To Christ I commend my soul. Jesu, receive my soul . . .' Then the sword fell and severed that slender neck as though it were the stem of a flower.

It was customary for the headsman to take the traitor's head and hold it aloft, by the hair, crying, 'So perish all traitors.' Perhaps the headsman from Calais was ignorant of the custom. Anne's women recovered the head from the straw, wrapped it with the body in a cloth and used an old arrow-box as a coffin. For this body, so long the lodestar of Henry's desire, the matrix from which the great Elizabeth had been hewn, this crowned and anointed Queen of England, no proper coffin had been prepared. With no ceremony Anne was buried in the little Church of St Peter ad Vincula, part of the Tower complex.

Where was Henry? Where was Jane Seymour? How one hates to contradict a highly popular and long-cherished tale. Henry was said to have been at Richmond, ready mounted, awaiting the boom of the gun from the Tower which would announce that he was a free man at last; he was said to have cried, 'Loose the hounds and away', and set out for Wiltshire, for Wolf Hall where the wedding-feast was already being prepared, and where on the next day he was to be married. The idea of the wedding bakemeats already in the oven at the moment when Anne died has a macabre fascination, but it must be discarded. As soon as he knew that Anne was dead, Henry, dressed all in white, stepped into his barge and was rowed to the riverside house in which he had installed Jane when he found Sir Nicholas Carew's house rather too far from the centre of things. Next day they went early to Hampton Court and were married there on 30 May.

12

The Legend Lives On

But ask not bodies doom'd to die
To what abode they go:
Since knowledge is but sorrow's spy
It is not safe to know.

Sir William Davenant (1608–68)

In the countryside memories are long, and until this century of instant entertainment, old stories were cherished and handed on. One such claims that Anne Boleyn lies buried in Salle Church under a slab of plain black marble, near to the known tomb of her grandparents: and in an Essex church a similar black slab is said to mark the place where her body rested overnight on its journey from London to Norfolk.

We know that Thomas Wyatt wrote, 'God provided for her corpse sacred burial, even in a place as it were consecrate to innocence.'

If her remains were moved it is more than likely that he and his sister organized the removal. It would have been relatively easy; the Tower officials would be relaxing from the vigilance of the last nineteen days and the snatching away of the body of a person executed for treason was not so usual a thing as to be guarded against. An ordinary cart with two men would attract little attention in a place where deliveries of food and fuel were constantly made. The paving-stone near the choir in the little church would not yet have settled into place, and an old arrow-box would be far less conspicuous than a coffin. In May the light lasts long. The cart could have reached Thornden Heath, those with it could have sheltered overnight in the church there – the functions of churches in Tudor times were far less specialized than they are nowadays. And a better place for a secret burial at the journey's end than Salle Church could hardly be desired; it stands in splendid isolation, well away from the village. If indeed Anne did have sacred burial there, the services of a priest would be

OPPOSITE The statue of Anne on the staircase at Blickling Hall needed but priests were, of all people, best skilled in the keeping of secrets.

Certainly, the legend was rooted and grew and stayed lively until well into the middle of the present century.

It might seem to be contradicted by a discovery made in November 1876, when some repair work was being done to the old church within the Tower of London. A paving-stone near the Choir where Anne was supposed to lie was lifted then and a skeleton revealed; and it is somehow typical of Anne's controversial and mysterious story that at a time when archaeological curiosity and enterprise was almost at its peak, Schliemann hunting for Troy, and Pompeii already excavated and some remnants of Greek culture rescued by Lord Elgin, nobody took much interest in the bones which may or may not have been Anne's. 'A medical man, assisting at the work' said he judged them to be 'the bones of a woman aged between twenty-five and thirty, and of delicate frame. The neck vertebrae especially small.' What a lost opportunity! A girl above average height, crammed into an arrow-box; did her head lie beside her? Without identity, without ceremony, the bones were buried again. Understandable; Queen Victoria was on the throne and monarchy had become very moral. Victoria was known not to set much store on her Tudor ancestry, preferring her Stuart blood, though the one derived from the other.

And the delicate bones may well have been those of Catherine Howard – she was much of Anne's build.

Can ghosts give evidence? Anne is said to haunt Hever in completely traditional style, a white, almost transparent phantom, drifting across a lawn. Blickling Hall had a ghost, known as Old Bullen, and one room, called 'Old Bullen's Study', had something about it so eerie and uncanny that even those supposed to clean it would not go inside. So it was locked and abandoned; but which room it was, what form the manifestation took, nobody now remembers.

Salle Church has a rather different story. The sexton there, a man of venerable age a quarter of a century ago and plainly a man of the utmost probity, showed me, an anonymous tourist, the black marble slab. I would have dug it up with my bare fingers. I asked had it ever been lifted, and was told that the patron of the church was not in favour of any investigation. The population of the village being three hundred and the

LEFT The brass to Sir Thomas Bullen at Hever Church
OPPOSITE Church of St Peter and St Paul, Salle, Norfolk where Anne is said to have been given a sacred burial

Virginal reputed to have belonged to Anne Boleyn

church the size of a small cathedral, the necessity for a patron, and of humouring his whim, was understandable.

'But she could be there,' the sexton admitted. 'She's said to walk here. Every year. At night on the 19th of May.' The precision of the dating shows how strong and lively the legend had been. 'But that's just a tale,' he said. 'I know because I once set out to prove it.'

He then told me a tale, all the stranger because he had no notion of its importance. Once, years ago, he had kept vigil on the night of the 19 May, and had seen nothing except a great hare which seemed to come from nowhere – he was sure he'd shut the door behind him. It led him, he said, a fine chase, jumping over the pews, twisting and turning. Then he stubbed his toe on the base of the font and when he recovered his balance the hare had vanished.

Everything about him, especially the dialect which I have spared you, proclaimed him to be a true Norfolk man; yet when I said, 'Well, she was supposed to be a witch, you know', he asked blankly what that had got to do with it? I had the pleasure of telling him that a hare was one of the shapes that a witch was supposed to be able to take at will, which is one

reason why many Norfolk people would have to be very near starvation before they would eat hare meat. He had never heard *that* one, he said. So he had regarded his ghost-hunt as a failure, and had told his tale in all innocence. It left me wondering . . .

How typical of a woman who loved a joke, who enjoyed masquerades, who had led another man a fine chase, to make a brief reappearance, not as a headless spectre or as a whole one, self-pitying and woebegone, but as an animal, beautiful and lively – and as elusive as ever.

The site of Anne's execution with St Peter ad Vincula in the background

Illustration Acknowledgments

Index